Will the real
KING ARTHUR
please stand up?

ALSO BY RONALD MILLAR

Hemingway
Kut: Death of an Army
Mata Hari
The Piltdown Men
A Time of Cherries

Will the real KING ARTHUR please stand up?

RONALD MILLAR

CASSELL
LONDON

CASSELL LTD.
35 Red Lion Square, London WC1R 4SG
and at sydney, Auckland, Toronto, Johannesburg,
an affiliate of
Macmillan Publishing Co., Inc.,
New York.

First published 1978

ISBN 0 304 30064 0

Typeset by Inforum Ltd., Portsmouth
Printed in Great Britain by
Billing & Son Ltd.,
Guildford, Surrey

Contents

1 At the mouth of the river which is called Glein

'Monsieur, your dog has stolen my knickers!' I could not believe my ears. There must be something wrong, some breakdown in communication, but I could not think what it could be. I understood the French language well enough, even spoke it with the same Breton hayseed accent used by the old lady. But there could be no mistaking the outrage in my accuser's voice or the emotion which rippled the fat on her powerful arms. The look she was giving me from under the lace coif would have withered a bed of stinging nettles.

I had climbed up through the copse from the river. Although it was still early March the narrow path was already overgrown with young ferns and there were patches of bluebells and daffodils everywhere. You could even hear the horse-chestnut buds bursting in the general tumult of spring. A pair of chaffinches were flying tight circles in courting aerobatics. It would have been idyllic but for the angry old lady who had appeared from the trees ahead with the suddenness of the Demon King in the pantomime.

The misunderstanding could be quickly put right.

'But, madam, I do not own a dog,' I protested. The old lady threw her head back and made a braying sound clearly demonstrating that the art of cavalier laughing is not dead. She jerked a thumb behind me.

'Then pray tell me, monsieur, what is that animal?' she cackled.

One glance was enough. I realized with the weariness of a long sufferer I was once again the victim of the juxtaposition of unlikely events. I seemed to have a dog all right, a large, brown, nasty-looking brute, and there was no mistaking the nature of the garment dangling by one leg from its jaws. And I thought I knew what had prompted the accusation.

I had seen the old lady pounding away at her laundry in the granite walled *lavoir* by the river bank and she had been having trouble with a dog which seemed fascinated by the proceedings. I had watched the mêlée through my binoculars, and although I had not heard what the old lady had been shouting, from her gestures I could guess she was not offering it biscuits. Then her sharp eyes had seen me up the slope and she had shouted something at me. I had felt it time to leave.

I should not have been surprised at the speed which the old lady had climbed the slope and cut off my retreat. You can't avoid old Breton ladies once they've decided to have a close look at you. Try going round by another road and once again they will appear in your path. Despite advanced age they seem to be able to move like ante-lopes. Once I was chased up the Lervily quay by one. It was all to do with horseplay with some other fishermen. I had inadvertently hit her on the back of her coif with a mackerel head. My flight had been hampered by rubber boots but she had been wearing heavy wooden clogs. She had overtaken me before I could reach the safety of the fish store and delivered a blow which had numbed my arm for hours.

But my latest adversary gave me a chance of escape. With a scream of rage she suddenly darted past me at the dog which fled down the path. I dashed to the top of the hill. I could still hear her trumpeting something about reporting me to the gendarmes when I reached the road.

As I retraced my steps to the town of Arzal I mused that this was hardly the stuff of archaeological enquiry. I am not yet given to steal-ing old lady's knickers and I certainly would not have journeyed several hundred kilometres through the north-west of France to do it. In fact I was looking for the most absorbing and elusive character in British history — King Arthur.

Most of us brought up on a diet of Alfred Lord Tennyson and Sir Walter Scott have a ready mental picture of King Arthur. He was a chivalrous, benign, Christian gentleman, husband of the faithless Guinevere, who presided with wisdom over his Round Table at Camelot, a table so designed that none of his knights would feel that he was superior to another.

Arthur would have been tall and straight, with fair hair and a beard. He wore a white surcoat over his shining armour and carried a shield, both emblazoned with the Red Cross of Saint George. He bat-tled on horseback with a lance and wielded a magic sword called Excalibur. With his knights he righted wrongs, rescued virtuous dam-sels in distress, and quested for the Holy Grail.

In fact this kind of King Arthur is pure fiction and our mental image is probably of King Richard Coeur de Lion or even Saint George. He was given birth by courtesy of the medieval romances, and is too late in time by more than a thousand years.

The real Arthur, if there was ever one, was no fair Plantagenet but a dark Celt, a hairy, painted warrior to whom chivalry would have been a weakness, and if he had mounted a horse he would have probably fallen off. Our Celt would have distressed more damsels than he rescued and only righted wrongs when it suited his purpose. He carried not a lance but a spear which according to Welsh legend had the chummy name of Ron but he did have a sword and this was called Caliburn.

So we have the curious case of a possibly real historical character becoming a fictional one. How could this have come about?

About the year 1136 a monk named Geoffrey of Monmouth wrote a history of the kings of Britain. Geoffrey came from Wales and in the Welsh mountains at that time were living a turbulent, wild, Celtic people, still free despite the invasions of the British Isles, whether Roman, Saxon, or the more recent Norman one. Geoffrey spoke Welsh and his countrymen had a strong tradition of narrative poetry and song which told the history of the land. It was to the bards that he went for some of his material. The bards could fill the Dark Ages, the long historical silence between the departure of the Romans up to the time of the Saxon monk, Bede, who being an extremely cautious historian rejected much of what he had heard of Celtic Britain.

Geoffrey's view of early British history was traditional and highly imaginative. For example, Britain's first king was made out to be a Trojan named Brutus and he invented spoof kings like Bladud who is supposed to have founded Bath and Lud who did the same for London. The monk held many other strange illusions. Three hundred years of military domination by the Romans seemed to him no more than a brief visit to see how we were. Geoffrey admits that the Saxon invasion was a major affair though he thought that its origin lay in three boatloads of mercenaries brought over from Scandinavia to fight the Scots, who decided they were being cheated out of rations and took it out on the neighbourhood, inviting their relatives over to join in the fun. At this point Geoffrey dips into his Welsh legends and brings out Arthur. Now he warms to his subject.

According to Geoffrey, Arthur was born at Tintagel in Cornwall as bastard son of lusty King Uther Pendragon and someone else's queen whose husband he impersonates to raid the marital bed with the aid of a spell cast by Merlin the Wizard. One must not be too surprised at magical happenings in Celtic legend. Sex changes, animals changing into men, and men into nothing at all, are its very essence. Failure to include at least one such transformation would have the bard leaving at speed wearing his harp for a collar.

Arthur comes to the throne in tender youth and wages war against the invading Saxons with a marvellous sword forged in the fairy Island of Avalon, bringing off a massive victory at Bath which brings peace for twelve years. The young king continues his victorious campaign in Ireland, Scotland, the Orkney Islands, Iceland and Norway. His headquarters were at Caerleon in Wales. Geoffrey did not invent the story of the Round Table but there was a brotherhood of knights which included Kay, Bedevere, and Lot who had a son called Gawain.

Arthur now takes his conquering army across the Channel to Gaul, now France, even marching on Rome but he hears of a revolt against him by his nephew Mordred and he returns to Cornwall where he fights his final battle. Arthur receives a mortal wound and he is taken to Avalon for a cure but to no avail. Our hero dies in about the year A.D. 542 and he leaves his crown to a kinsman. Now the Saxons tear the island to pieces and Geoffrey closes his history. But he does have a lot of material left over and he adds a long poem about the life of Merlin and Arthur's last journey to Avalon which is also called the Isle of the Blest and is in distant seas.

Very much impressed by the monk's tale of the wonderful king was a man of no less metal himself, King Henry II of England. This great autocrat ruled from the Cheviots to the Pyrenees but he felt far from secure. His realm was so vast that a large number of his subjects thought he had no right to be there. Henry had come to the throne only after a long and bitter struggle between his mother, Matilda, daughter of Henry I, and King Stephen. So destructive was this civil war that the country was close to ruin and only battle fatigue forced an agreement between the warring factions which allowed Stephen to continue on the throne until his death, on the condition that Matilda's eldest son succeeded him as Henry II.

So as founder of the new Plantagenet dynasty Henry had a permanent twitch. He was constantly looking behind him for the assassin's knife or revolt. The throne was only his by combat and he could lose it in the same way. It must have been one of those queer quirks of the medieval mind that persuaded Henry he might have less to fear if he could show that Arthur was buried in his realm and not some other country.

And so it was put about that while travelling in Wales Henry had been told by an 'imprudent' bard that Glastonbury in what we now call Somerset was in fact the old Isle of Avalon. In fact it had never been called anything of the kind. In Celtic times it was Ynyswitrin but the whole story is so much in line with Henry's aspirations that it must have been a Plantagenet fabrication. So the monks at the Benedictine monastery were ordered to find the body.

And they did, but they took too long about it. The monks must have known that Henry had little patience with ecclesiastical triflers from what had happened to Archbishop Thomas Becket, butchered at the high altar at Canterbury. Perhaps the monks did not take Henry seriously, or maybe they could not decide what the grave of the long dead Celtic king should look like. The delay could not have been due to scruples over honesty for Glastonbury was at the top of the league for finding or providing holy relics to attract a constant stream of rich pilgrims to the abbey.

Splinters of wood from the True Cross or from the table used at the Last Supper and the finger bones of saints were to be found at most of the great European religious houses. But Glastonbury always went several better. Not only did the abbey claim to be the earliest religious establishment in Britain, built by Saint Joseph of Arimathea, the disciple who took Jesus down from the cross on the Hill of Skulls, but boasted the graves of no less than three important saints, Patrick of Ireland, David of Wales, and Gildas of Brittany. Even the Holy Grail was said be among the abbey treasures.

We should not be too critical of such tricks. The monks had to eat and if the pilgrims went away better men then what was the harm in it all? What is important is that this demonstrates that Glastonbury was quite capable of pulling off one of history's biggest archaeological frauds and to such effect that even today it is widely believed that the abbey was the final resting place of King Arthur.

By now Henry was an old man and he was determined to have roots before he died. One night a mysterious fire razed the abbey to the ground. Henry got his wish. Some accounts say the the final act of his life was the visit to Glastonbury where he gazed in wonder at the bones of his distant forerunner. But it is more generally accepted that it was Henry's successor, England's popular but normally absent king, Richard Coeur de Lion, the second Plantagenet, who made the pilgrimage.

The monks were probing between a pair of stone columns, ran the contemporary account, when they came across a stone slab which informed them in Latin:

'Here lies buried famous King Arthur in the Isle of Avalon'.

Another nine feet down was a huge coffin made from the trunk of an oak tree. Inside was the skeleton of a giant of a man, the skull damaged to prove that he had died of battle wounds. Better still, in the coffin were some finer bones and a hank of yellow hair, undoubtedly the remains of Arthur's Queen Guinevere.

The monks had responded magnificently but the enthusiasm for the discovery overlooked certain aspects of the burial which were, to say the least, odd. Burials in graves of the kind found at Glastonbury had not been thought of as long ago as halfway through the sixth century when Geoffrey said Arthur had died. The debased Roman uncials of the Latin inscription were fine for A.D. 1190, the year of the discovery, but certainly not much before. And it seemed ridiculous to add the place of burial when it was under the monks' feet. Nevertheless the bones were received with joy, anyway it was extremely unhealthy to snigger where the Plantagenet will was concerned.

Long before the Glastonbury find and despite the absence of remains, Arthur was already being built into a flourishing industry. The collection of stories with Arthur as the central theme was required reading at court. Another Welshman, Walter de Mapp, sent Arthur wandering over land and sea questing the Holy Grail. To the noble band of knights he added fearless Sir Galahad, the flower of chivalry, without a blot on his escutcheon.

So far the tales had been written in Latin but now a Norman monk named Robert Wace translated them into French verse. His *Roman de Brut* was an adaptation of Geoffrey but with even more poetic invention and licence. He gave the Round Table to the world. He wired myth, legend, and tradition together to produce a work which was immensely popular. Wace was translated into English by a cleric named Layamon.

The most creative writer of Arthurian stories, however, was Chrétien de Troyes, resident dream spinner at Poitou where Henry's unwanted queen waited at her private court for the summons to England that never seemed to come. Chretien dressed his warriors in medieval armour and featured them in long verse romances about knights errant, courtly love, combat, damsels in distress, and derring-do, where good was always triumphant and evil a bad bet. He sneaks Arthur's birthplace off from Cornwall to Angers, the heartland of the Plantagenets. His court was no longer at Caerleon but at Camelot in an unspecified country. To the Round Table he adds Lancelot, Eric, Cliges, Yvain, and Perceval, while from Lyonesse a legendary land which once lay off the Cornish coast, comes Sir Tristram who fell in love with his future aunt thus providing the Arthurian cycle with its greatest love story.

By now the Plantagenets had hoodwinked themselves, or were certainly behaving as if they had. Henry's grandson was christened Arthur. Richard generously presented Arthur's sword to Tancred of Sicily while on his way to Palestine for the Third Crusade. That Excalibur had been found was certainly not mentioned in the eye-witness account when the grave was opened. Nor was Sir Tristram's sword which was part of the treasure lost by Richard's wicked brother, John, when a change of tide almost drowned him when crossing the Wash. Meanwhile John had made a negative contribution by having Henry's grandson murdered, thus depriving England of a real King Arthur for the lad was in the direct line of succession.

When Edward I was trying to conquer the Welsh in A.D. 1275 he paid a much publicized visit to Glastonbury. The famous bones were put on show 'for the veneration of the people' then reburied before the great altar. Curiously the skull was removed and got lost. This desecration makes little sense other than Edward must have been in touch with another imprudent bard. The Welsh believed that Arthur was 'the once and future king', not really dead but slumbering all those years in a mountain cave. One day he would awake, said the prophecy, and drive the oppressors from Wales, and Edward knew who the bards had in mind. By losing the skull Edward was working a little magic on his own account. If an immortal Arthur did lead a rising its leader would be without a head.

Wearing King Arthur's crown, another unannounced discovery, Edward took his army to Scotland to prove his right to rule over the Scots, just as Arthur had done according to Geoffrey of Monmouth.

In A.D. 1331 yet another Plantagenet paid a royal visit to Glastonbury. The stunt this time was a seer named John Blome who Edward III hoped would find the remains of Joseph of Arimathea. According to an abbey tradition Joseph lay in a marble coffin which would one day be discovered and would be the marvel of visitors from all over the world, a prophecy which must have made the monks rattle their collection boxes in anticipation. The Holy Grail had by now become two silver cruets containing the blood and sweat of Jesus Christ. These also must be found. But the search was in vain. One can imagine the monks sleeping by their firebuckets for many a night thereafter but Edward must have been preoccupied with other matters.

But all this is Plantagenet propaganda, no doubt given impetus by the fervour in noble quarters for the Crusades, a kind of earthly prepayment for a place in Paradise purchased by driving the Saracens from the Holy Land. What of the real Celtic Arthur written about by Geoffrey of Monmouth and now so changed by the romancers as to be hardly recognisable? All the helpful legends from the part of Celtic Britain that came to be called England vanished along with the language after the Saxon conquest. But there still survives a faint hint of what Geoffrey's long vanished sources might have been like.

Arthur or his companions frequently appear in the Welsh *triads*. These are three stories linked together by a similar theme to aid the teller's memory. Arthur was one of *The Three Red Rangers* and *The Three Frivolous Bards*. He digs up the head of Bran, a talisman against invasion, and so is guilty of one of *The Three Wicked Uncoverings*. Other *triads* mention Arthur's treacherous nephew Medraut, not exactly Geoffrey's Mordred but still recognisable, and Arthur's queen, or rather queens for with typical Celtic generosity he is given three, all named Gwenhwyvaer, again recognisable as Guinevere. Medraut rapes one of the Gwenhwyvaers during a raid on Arthur's castle at Kelliwic in Cornwall and conspires with the Saxons to bring about Arthur's fatal battle. Arthur appears to be far from the Christian character painted by the romancers, always being mixed up in disreputable activities such as cattle rustling and tumbles in bed.

The earliest reference to Arthur in a poem, not a story, comes as a fleeting aside in the collection called the *Gododdin*. Although these poems are in the Welsh language they are thought to have been composed in Cumberland in the sixth century and intended as elegies for a number of warriors slain in a series of disastrous attacks on the Saxons at Catterick. Of one of the dead heroes the poet says that although he was brave 'he was not Arthur'. That was all.

A purely Welsh poem of around the eleventh century contains a fragment where the poet uses a favourite Celtic literary device to trot out his players. The warden at a city gate orders Arthur to name his companions before he lifts the bar. Arthur complies, recounting the exploits of some of them including Kei and Bedwyr, Kay and Bedevere of the romances. *The Black Book of Carmarthen* also mentions Arthur's son, Llacheu and alludes to a band which roams the West Country as 'Arthur's Men'. But Arthur is never referred to as a king but always as a leader of men, except on one occasion where he is described as a kind of emperor.

But the masterpiece of survival is the collection of tales called the *Mabinogion*, thought to be so ancient that they pre-date Geoffrey of Monmouth. One of them entitled *Culhwch and Olwen* recounts how Prince Culhwch (pronounced Kilhooch with a throat clearing on the 'ch') develops a passion for Olwen, daughter of the giant Ysbaddaden, who does not think much of the match. Accordingly the prince seeks the aid of Arthur and his men and one can't imagine a more strange collection. They include Saint Gildas and the famous bard Taliesin and a number of other characters with strange powers, such as Ear who could hear an ant rising in the morning from fifty miles away, Tracker who could hunt a man down seven years before he was even born, and Drinker who swallowed entire seas to quench his thirst.

All the original Welsh material which mentions Arthur is of this fanciful kind and apart from the just as marvellous 'lives of the Celtic saints', into which the monks occasionally drag Arthur as a swashbuckling and unruly character, this would have been the sum total but for an amazing discovery made by a churchman at the beginning of the nineteenth century.

The Rev. William Gunn was fossicking in the Vatican archives when he happened across a volume containing a large number of miscellaneous manuscripts. One was a short history of Britain written in the ninth century by a monk named Nennius. Gunn could hardly believe his good fortune. For ten folio pages the war horns scattered the dust of the library. Arthur was alive and well and living in Rome.

Nennius confessed to having 'thrown together' a large number of earlier manuscripts to produce his history, probably the remains of despoiled religious libraries. He lists twelve battles in which the British were victorious against the Saxons and the 'magnanimous commander' in all these encounters was Arthur, not a king but a *dux bellorum*, a leader in battles.

'And though there were many more noble than himself yet he was twelve times chosen as their commander and was often conqueror,' comments the monk.

According to Nennius the first of Arthur's victories was 'at the mouth of the river called Glein'. The next four were 'upon a river called Dubglas in the region of Linnius'. The sixth was 'on the river called Bassas'. The seventh was 'in the forest of Celidon'. The eighth was 'by Castle Guinnion'. The ninth was 'at the City of the Legion'. The tenth was 'on the banks of the river which is called Tribruit'. The eleventh was 'on the hill called Agned'. And the twelfth was 'on Mount Badon'.

Nennius did not mention Arthur's unlucky thirteenth battle, said by Welsh tradition to have been fought at Camlann, nevertheless Gunn's discovery was received with great enthusiasm and was no doubt responsible for the Arthurian revival by the authors of *Idylls of the King* and *The Lady of the Lake*. Not only English writers but writers in the United States, France, Germany, and Italy joined in the literary fanfare. But there was also a discordant note, faint at first but growing rapidly louder and becoming raspberry flavoured. The historians were at each other's throats. Nobody seemed to be able to find even one of Arthur's battlefields or if they did someone questioned its validity.

The 'Glein' might be the Lincolnshire or Lancashire Glen. The 'forest of Celidon' might be the ancient forest of Caledonia as Scotland was once called, and the 'Tribruit' might also be up there somewhere. 'The City of the Legion' was obviously Chester, Caerleon or York for these were the only cities in Britain which the Romans made their headquarters. But which one? Geoffrey of Monmouth had indicated Bath as the scene of the greatest British victory so this must be 'Mount Badon'. 'Camlann' might have something to do with the River Cam in Somerset or in Cornwall. But as for 'Bassas' or 'Dubglas', 'Castle Guinnion' and 'the hill of Agned' hands are thrown up in despair.

These associations are highly controversial and just one small objection to them is that they seem too widespread to carry conviction as a military campaign conducted by a single commander. Against this view it might be argued that Arthur's enemies were out for pillage rather than permanent occupation and being seafarers were likely to turn up where wind and tide took them. But other frustrated authorities said that the battles were just twelve, that Nennius or some predecessor had snatched out of the air and lumped together, attributing them to Arthur for convenience or to make a good story. Some said Nennius himself was non-existent and another monkish prank, even that some Saxon wrote the manuscript. Another suspect was 'Mark the Anchorite' who had edited or copied Nennius's original.

But there was already in existence another source which confirmed what Geoffrey and Nennius had said about the victory over the Saxons at Mount Badon. This was the sixth century outburst by the querulous monk, Saint Gildas, a very real and live character who appears as a fictional prop in the *Mabinogion*.

Gildas set out, at least his title said so, to write a history of the destruction and conquest of Britain by the Saxons. Unfortunately after a cool start the monk loses his temper and the work degenerates into a withering attack on Celtic chiefs who fiddled and worse while Britain was put to the fire and the axe. At times old Gildas gets completely out of hand.

Bodicea, Britain's most famous warrior queen, was for irascible Gildas a tyrant and a deceitful lioness always engaged in plunder and rapine. Constantine was a tyrannical whelp and a blasphemer. Aurelius Caninus was foul and swallowed up in the filthiness of horrible murder. Voteporix was a foolish tyrant and a spotted leopard in manners and mischief. Cuneglasus had 'fallen into filth and naughtiness'. And Maglocunus was soaked in the wine of the Sodommitical grape!

But in one of the monk's less heated passages, no doubt to contrast the evil of the other tyrants, Gildas tells of the brave leader Ambrosius Aurelianus ('even he was a violent man', snaps Gildas to keep his hand in) who led a successful British counter attack. Then came a series of defeats and victories for either side culminating in the greatest British victory of all which brought peace and order for a generation. This victorious encounter was at Mount Badon, Arthur's victory according to Nennius. Oddly enough Gildas omits to mention the name of the leader and some historians take this to mean that the victory could also be attributed to Ambrosius. The argument against this doubting faction is that Gildas's battles covered a lengthy period and Badon comes too late for Ambrosius, and Geoffrey of Monmouth had put a massive victory in the reign of his 'King' Arthur.

But how did I come to be looking for Arthur in Brittany? I will beat myself over the head with the biggest club first. I had been living in Brittany quite a long time before I began to suspect that Arthur might have been a Breton so I'm wide open to the attack that as I was living there I might as well look there as anywhere else. As I am playing prosecutor to my own defendant I concede that the point was made brilliantly and confess that this was in fact the case. But I must add that if I had been living in China I would not have bothered. Brittany seemed to me a very likely place to discover Arthur.

I began to look in Brittany not because Geoffrey of Monmouth had written that Arthur had warred in Gaul but because it is a hallowed tradition of the Dark Ages that the Bretons are the descendants of British refugees who fled there from the British Isles. The emigration is thought to have taken place between the first Saxon raids up until the time when the island was finally overrun, betweeen the fifth and seventh centuries. The language spoken in modern Brittany, like Welsh, descends from the language spoken in Britain over a thousand years ago.

Even in these days of overcrowding, Brittany is still a lonely backwater of big skies and great silences, a kind of island isolated by the Atlantic to the west, and to the east by a railway and road transport system that never seems to go where you want it to. It is also a Celtic land with the same kind of bardic traditions as Wales. This is ideal country for the preservation of legends.

I had heard — I had not been told — that the Bretons also had a tradition of a mighty warrior who defended them against the Saxons. His name was Arzur. The old people who might talk about such things are shy and finding him was not going to be easy. Instead he found me.

Brittany is a granite country, at the same time wild but soft, a kind of untrodden Cornwall. Its appeal, or lack of it, is very much according to the individual taste or disposition, like mountains are loved by some while others are oppressed by them. It has the perpendicular cliffs of the Lizard or Cape Wrath, the beaches of Sussex or Miami and the interior has the gentleness of the Sussex Downs or the Weald of Kent. Like their land the people are a mixture, warm but aloof, superficially friendly but brooding and deep. The brash cannot fault them as jolly chaps, the sensitive call them remote, the neurotic find them spooky. Someone told me that the Bretons reminded her of cats, although they did not look much like them. I have thought about this analogy a good deal and there is a lot to it.

I had lived a long time by the Brittany shore and seen the hot beaches of summer change into the misty wastelands of winter, the bikinis and chocolate glacées substituted by weeping sandpipers searching amongst the debris of the Biscayan storms at the tide's ending. Alone in such a place perhaps a stranger begins to discern the pulse of Brittany. Then the monuments of a long dead people, the standing stones and the grave markers, seem to gather the land back to themselves. In high summer they are interesting things to point walking sticks at but when the sun has gone south they exude a dampness which creeps into your soul. You keep clear of them.

On a dark evening you try to concentrate on something else, not what made the last inexplicable sound near the head of the wooden ladder to the attic. The wind throbbing across the roof becomes hushed whispers or the wings of demons.

To delay the loneliness of night I would stroll down to Tante-'phine's, the only place in the hamlet that offered a glass of wine and a chat. It was always warm from the bread oven and you usually found someone you knew or a stranger attracted like yourself by the prospect of companionship. There might be the crew of the *Perle des Vagues* late up from the quay, or the card players having finished their game might hang about for gossip. These evenings held a kind of magic for me. I listened but seldom joined in for to do so would break the spell, remind the talkers of the presence of an interloper. If it did the conversation would return to the stuff of tourism like it did in the summer, for Celts need little encouragement to perform in a generally accepted Celtic way for tourists.

I had been part of the hamlet long enough not to be thought a suitable audience for play acting. I had worked with the fishermen and dressed like they did in faded and patched cotton smock and trousers. This was not for effect but a sensible and economical form of dress. But I must admit I wore my *'glazics'* more like a badge of honour, for I had earned the privilege off the Azores in the Breton tunny boats, the cruellest and most arduous experience of my life. But I have written all about that in *A Time of Cherries*.*

I had earned my innocuity and the men talking over their wine no longer took much notice of me. And I understood Breton well enough for them to ignore me. The frequent translations into French of my earlier days at Lervily ruined the flow of conversation. To hear the language of the British Isles of over a thousand years ago is like stepping from a time machine. It is a language of loud whispers, of

*Published by Cassell Ltd. 1977.

faint buzzes in the throat, a cigarette in the mouth kind of language. It also has some powerful explosives and to be sworn at in Breton makes your eyes water. But by now the novelty had worn off and as often as not I drifted off into an introspective reverie, allowing the conversation to stimulate or otherwise, according to the current mental preoccupation.

It was on such an evening when the rain was threatening to burst the window panes at Tante'phines's that the word 'Camelot' crashed into the haze of my mind and nearly snapped my neck with the speed it lifted my chin from the glass. Could I have misheard? Were the fishermen talking about the long searched for court of King Arthur of the romances? Unlikely, but as I hadn't heard the conversation I could not be sure.

'Who said that?' I asked, trying not to appear too eager for the Breton loves secrets as much as he does his wine. They are a kind of currency in a small village, and big ones too, where everything is common knowledge, where one is born, lives, and dies in the same cottage, and marries the nearest available girl or boy up the road.

'Who said what?' snapped my friend Fayot. 'Fayot' in Breton means 'beans' on which the Marine Nationale is alleged to subsist. The old man had the temper of a master-at-arms at times.

'Camelot,' I replied. 'Where's that?'

The Bretons are transparent when it comes to facial expressions. When he is trying to cheat you he puts on a cunning expression worthy of the villain in an old time melodrama. The look common to all the now silent talkers at the table was one of astonishment, complete with wide eyes and gaping jaws.

'Someone just said "Camelot" and I just wondered where it was,' I said, as casually as possible.

But old Fayot of the uneven temper was in no mood for me. Red wine, and the talkers had consumed large quantities of it that evening, makes one liverish.

'That's not looking at you,' he shouted quivering with rage. 'Mind your own business.' I had broken the spell. The talkers swigged off their wine and left in an angry clatter of clogs. I distinctly heard the word 'Yann-Saoz' and knew that this meant me. 'Saoz' means 'Saxon' and it used for nasty things by the Bretons. 'Kranket-Saoz', for example are small crabs loved by gourmets but when tangled up in fishing nets in large numbers they cause a lot of extra work. And despite their size they pinch so hard that you have to use bad language. Maybe that's how they got their name for the expletive I used to cover the contingency was Saxon in origin. The British Isles for the Bretons is *'Bro-Saoz'* meaning 'the land of the Saxons'. This illustrates the impact these terrible warriors had on the Bretons for I've never heard the description used politely.

But my temporary unpopularity was worth it, I thought. I had stumbled accidentally into the Celtic dream world, guarded secrets never spoken of before a stranger. I was sure now that Camelot existed somewhere in Brittany and with patience I would find it without native help.

Back at the cottage I lit my oil lamp and got out my maps of Brittany. It was not exactly the kind of collection that has museums writing to you in the hope you will leave it to them when you die. One old map was an illustrated picture postcard. Another had been copied from the sleeve of a long playing record. I had never been able to trace the originals.

For the time being I neglected my older maps. If the Fayot clique knew the place so well then Camelot should be quite close and the best map I had of the locality was a modern Michelin 1/200,000 scale motoring version that could be bought at any service station. I was looking for a name perhaps a thousand years old and more, but place names have not changed as much in Brittany as they have in Britain. The Bretons call their villages by names that have to make sense for their language is very much alive.

Take for example Pendennis, near Falmouth, Cornwall, which means nothing in English and vexes tourists as to who the Dennis might be that the village was named for. They could be told that Dennis was once a local chief or that he kept a brothel for pirates. In fact Pendennis in the dead Cornish language, a language similar to Breton, is *'Pen an innes'* meaning headland with the island.

My task was of course complicated by the fact that my map was produced not by the Bretons but by travelling Frenchmen who could neither speak the language nor had the ear for it. The French are incapable of catching the nuances of Breton and they would have written down only what they thought they had heard. And they certainly could not repeat the names correctly. A Parisian friend who tried several times to pronounce 'Aber Wrac'h' had to go and sit down until he felt better. I remember that at the time I was quite confident that I would find Camelot somewhere in Brittany. The chance mention of the place at Tante'phine's had merely jolted together an idea which had been forming in my mind for some time. My reasoning ran like this. Although Arthur was a creature of Welsh legends these seldom locate him in Wales but push him off to Cornwall, suggesting he was not really a Welsh hero but more likely Cornish. Apart from Tintagel, which like Glastonbury's 'Avalon' was never called that in Arthur's time, none of the Arthurian sites and certainly none of his battles have been identified there. And this is the one place in England where the old Celtic names might have survived. The Saxons were not much interested in Cornwall and the old language was still in general use until the eighteenth century.

I had discovered that there was another Cornwall. 'Cornwall' is an age-corrupted description meaning 'West Wales' — better, 'the west country of the foreigners'. The north-west portion of Brittany was also at one time 'West Wales'. The Celtic version is 'Kernow' or 'Kernew' — the old name for both Britain's Cornwall and Brittany's Cornwall. This name survives on old Breton maps as 'Bro Kerne' meaning 'the West Country'. The French use the old Frankish version and call it 'Cornailles', pronounced 'Cornwaie'.

Angry old Saint Gildas certainly raves about 'British' tyrants but the old inhabitants of Brittany would also have been called 'British' for there was no alternative description. Even today the Bretons describe their country as 'Breizh Izel' or 'Lower Britain'. No wonder the Saxon and Norman scholars were confused about what country the Welsh legends had in mind. It is not unlikely then that when the monks wrote about the British and the Welsh bards sang about Cornwall they meant, to use modern terms, the Bretons and Brittany.

Brittany has a stronger claim to Arthur. Geoffrey of Monmouth, although descended on his mother's side from the kings of Wales, attributed his story of Arthur's last journey to Avalon not to Welsh but to Breton bards. Another of his sources is reputed to be Rhys ap Tewdor, a Welshman who spent most of his life exiled in Brittany. The Norman Robert Wace wrote that he got his story of the Round Table from Bretons. He even visited Brittany to get additional material. Many of the names of Arthur's knights are reckoned by Celtic scholars to be Breton in origin. The Arthurian tale in *The Mabinogion* is Breton, in fact only two tales in the entire collection are thought to be Welsh, the rest could only have come from Brittany.

But how had the Arthurian legends arrived in Wales? In Arthurian times Wales was beset on all sides. The Saxons had overrun most of what we now call England. The Scots, then a recently arrived tribe from Ireland, and their Pictish allies were pushing southward, looting and burning. The Irish were making piratical raids across the Irish Sea. Wales was an island in a sea of foreign conquest. Another was Brittany where the Gauls lived and because the Gauls themselves were being jammed against the Atlantic coast by the Franks they fought back lustily at the Saxon attempts to gain a foothold on their land. For the Welsh then Arthur's victories were a message of hope. Both were a seafaring people and there was much interchange between the two similar nations and, importantly, they had, and have, a common language. Maybe, it was thought, Arthur would come to their deliverance.

I was still working through the map when Fayot dropped in next morning, coughing significantly and complaining of a dry throat. I poured him a glass of wine then returned to my work. The old fisherman sat down beside me, watching the alchemy through his strange hooded Breton eyes. Bretons seem to have infinite patience. I can actually write with one in the room for they make no sound, and they seldom move unnecessarily. This gift makes them the finest fishermen in the world. But at length I rested back in my chair to ease my back and lit a cigarette. I offered one to Fayot which he accepted without a word. Bretons don't give vocal thanks for things. They say it by widening the eyelids slightly. When they do say 'thanks' they do so with such force and vigour that it sounds like a joke and it usually is. Seeing I was temporarily unoccupied Fayot allowed his curiosity to come into the open.

'You are planning a journey, perhaps?' he asked politely.

'No. I'm looking for Camelot,' I replied, putting some powdered glass in 'Camelot' for I hadn't quite forgiven Fayot for his tantrum of the previous evening.

'What do you mean "looking for camelote"? I don't understand you.'

'Is that so?' I said tartly. 'You were talking about the place last evening.'

'Camelote, you say?'

'I do'.

The old man began to chuckle softly in an annoying way.

'You have crabs in the head then. You will not find a place called camelote.'

'So you say. Then why do you speak of a place when it does not exist? Maybe it is you who have crabs in the head.'

'Perhaps I have.' Fayot was enjoying himself, immensely, chuckling louder than ever, his eyes watering. 'Crabs in the head you say, but not as many as you, camelote is not a place. It is something you buy which is not worth the money. Rubbish, that's what we call *"camelote"*. It's a French expression but we use it in Breton. Ho—ho—ho. Ha—ha—ah. Just fancy spending a whole night looking for camelote. Just wait till I tell them at the café.'

Very funny. But I was not as dismayed as I might have been by Fayot's mundane explanation. Shortly after two o'clock that morning I had found one of Arthur's missing battlefields. It was not very long before I found all the rest.

So far my Arthurian map hunt and reading had been confined to spare time. I got at it when I could. My writing took me to the United States and I found some more Arthur there. I remember thinking it was odd that a Scot living in France was researching an English king at a Californian library using material written in English by a Welsh professor at the University of Chicago.

I would have to visit the battlefields one day. Not that I hoped to find anything startling like Caliburn or Ron or even bones. That would be for serious archaeology and beyond my means. But I did hope to catch some of the colour and shape of Arthur. For no other reason than 'why not?' I would trace Arthur's campaign in the sequence used by Nennius.

It was also to be a sentimental journey. I was saying good-bye, paying a respectful farewell to a people with whom I had spent no small part of my life, not always a time of happiness, but of great happiness too, with times of vexation, frustration and downright misery, which is just like anywhere else and for anyone else. And so the next spring but one found me at Arthur's first battlefield.

I caught a taxi outside Redon railway station. Nennius had specified that Arthur's first victory had been at the mouth of the River Glein but he never said which bank. But Saxons did not land just to look at the scenery. There must have been some loot in the offing and Arthur would have been defending it. My Michelin map gave me a clue to what this might have been. On the northern bank was the site of a ruined monastery called Pen Lan. A monastery would have drawn Saxons like dogs to wet cement. I thought I would go there for a start.

'Nothing at Pen Lan but rubbish and a few stones,' the driver informed me as he accelerated past the speed of sound, the normal pace of Breton drivers which curls your toes in your boots.

'Why not go to Roche Bernard?' He was now steering with one finger.

'What's there?' I asked, trying to concentrate. The taxi narrowly missed an old man with a loaf of bread and my driver seemed disappointed.

'Nothing much, but it depends what you are after,' he said in an aggrieved tone.

This seemed like prying and how do you explain you are trying to find someone who died about fifteen hundred years ago? I had still not quite decided whether to be frank about my mission thus risk all kinds of invention or to keep quiet in the hope that something worthwhile might turn up. Silence had a lot to commend it. The other method seemed likely to put me in the madhouse. I would have to try both, and the taxi driver seemed a suitable subject for the frankness technique.

Coming from Redon he was hardly likely to spoil the scent at Pen Lan, even taking into account the highly efficient Breton grapevine.

'I'm looking for Arthur,' I informed him. I thought this was cunning. It gave no clue as to the kind of Arthur I was seeking. If he knew nothing of value he would conclude that Arthur was just someone living in the neighbourhood. It would be unlikely to unleash a spate of bogus information of the kind known in France as 'la tourisme' and in England 'kid 'em'. The driver shook his head. The name meant nothing to him. I thought I'd try the Breton version of the name.

'Arzur, perhaps, no?' The effect was instantaneous and almost catastrophic. The driver braked so violently I was all but moulded into the dashboard.

'Bullharst, why didn't you say so? You don't want Pen Lan,' he shouted excitedly. He turned the car in such a tight circle that it must have strained the chassis and we shot off back in the direction we had come. My ears were still buzzing with the 'bullharst', a Breton firecracker expletive of which no-one will tell me the meaning but I congratulated myself on my good fortune. This was going to be easier than I had ever anticipated.

We were racing down a narrow road with a surface so uneven as to suggest intensive bombardment. I could count the craters by the number of times my head struck the car roof. We shot through grey granite hamlets with quaint names like 'Green Pigeon' and 'Stag

Horn'. We flew even faster when he got a nun on an autocycle in his sights but she escaped by driving through a hedge into a field. Then to my intense chagrin we drew into the square of the village of Arzal. My Breton pronunciation was not as good as I had thought.

'One hundred francs, monsieur, not including the tip,' announced the driver. This was too much for a thirty kilometre journey. I hopefully offered him half and he took it so quickly that I got no satisfaction from the deal.

It was not far from Arzal to the river bank, about a half hour's walk, so I was content to forgo the monastery. And Arzal meant something. It was a kind of recollection of Arthur. Not a few experts are persuaded that Arthur may be an allusion to the Celtic bear god Artor. In Breton a bear is an '*arz*'. The bear god exemplifies both cunning and courage. Maybe on the banks of the Vilaine I had found a memory of the great warrior himself.

The river was now called the Vilaine but one of my old maps told me that in recent memory it had been called Gwilen. In identifying places from the Nennius list there is a further complication in addition to the changes wrought by the passage of time. The manuscript exists not as one but as a family of copies made by various monks during the eleventh and twelfth centuries. They differ widely. The 'Glein' was also referred as 'glemu', 'glem, and 'gem'. The two versions I used are considered to be the most respectable for their consistency and conformity to the Celtic language. These are the H and K manuscripts which differ little at all.

'Glein' then is the accepted spelling of the river at the mouth of which Arthur took on the Saxons for the first time. The name comes from the old Welsh word 'Glan' meaning 'pure' or 'clear'. In Breton 'Gwilen' comes from a similar root word and means exactly the same. It is pronounced 'goolen' which is so near the Welsh pronunciation as to make no difference. It was on the northern bank of the River Glein that on gazing through my binoculars I saw the old lady and the dog by the *lavoir*.

I must have been all of a kilometre towards Arzal before the old lady's cries died away. I began to wonder whether I had been the target of a local extortion racket of the 'pay for the knickers or I'll report you to the gendarmes' genre. Maybe the dog belonged to the old lady and had been specially trained. But something had gone wrong. I could imagine the old lady thrashing the dog with something sturdy like a table leg, or maybe a pick-axe. I could hear the whimpers as it went supperless to bed on sharp stones out in the cold yard. This thought gave me great pleasure.

I was disturbed by the rattle of claws on macadam. I thought at first it was the bear god himself. To my intense disgust it was the ghastly mongrel with the knickers. With a proprietary air he took up station just ahead of me trailing his banner of shame. I pelted him with stones and whacked at him with sticks but he would not go away. We were entering Arzal, passing villagers leaning on their gates to see they are not stolen. Bretons can roar with laughter without moving a facial muscle and I was given a splendid demonstration of the art.

I became suddenly aware of a little man walking beside me as if we had been companions for life. He had the aspect of a rummage sale. He was wearing a threadbare and faded black velvet jacket and striped morning trousers, both items many sizes too large, sleeves turned back at the wrists and the voluminous trouser legs folded into rubber boots. By contrast his second-hand beret was far too small and as though to give it an expansive appearance it was pulled down to his ear roots. His elfish, ill-shaven face had a studied solemnity.

'That couldn't be your dog, could it?' I asked. I can't remember that the little man made any reply at all but the impression I gained was that he did not know the animal. We shook hands formally and Henri examined his palm carefully before he thrust it back into his pocket where it was normally kept. This puzzled me, making me wonder whether to take the gesture as an insult or not.

He asked me where I came from and I told him. To my surprise Henri said that he also came from up my way. At present though he was working locally at Saint Gildas de Rhuys as a guide at the cathedral, or at least he had been until the *gendarmerie nationale* had told him to go away. Unofficial guides were not permitted, he was told by a fat gendarme. He must seek permission at the *mairie*. But the mayor had told him that it was the gendarmes who appointed the guides. Later the fat gendarme had caught him with a party of tourists and had chased him through the cathedral crying: 'Stop or I'll shoot.'

'That kind of language in the House of God, can you believe it possible?' Henri asked me earnestly.

The next day Henri had climbed to the roof of the square tower of Saint Gildas de Rhuys with a small bean can in which he had mixed some chalk and water. All that day he had peppered that gendarme who kept turning his red face heavenwards crying:

'*La merde . . . Les sales pigeons . . . Bullharst . . . Gaarst . .*' until one of the holy fathers had told him to be gone and wash his mouth out with carbolic soap. Honour thus satisfied and the gendarme punished for his blasphemy, Henri was now available for offers.

I noticed that Henri had an occasional stutter which he tried to disguise by dropping his voice to a deep bass which then rose of its own accord giving his phrases an exasperated tone at the end. I reasoned that this was why he had studied his palm before speaking. He was trying to take the stutter by surprise. Henri also had an unusual gait. He thrust his legs forward purposely, stiff at the knees, and gave the impression of a cat walking on ice.

He said he thought I spoke Breton rather well and I told him about the tunny boats. Henri had done that too, amongst other things like grape picking, farm hand and general expert. Henri could not remember the tunny boat's name nor did he give me much confidence that he had ever been aboard one. He was far too small although he did say he was cook. All this time I kept stoning the dog but Henri did not appear to see him.

We marched to the centre of Arzal and turned into a bistro as if by mutual consent. The *Madame* shot a hard look at my new friend as she served us the wine. After a token offer to pay which I found myself refusing Henri drank at my expense for the rest of the evening. I soon discovered that giving the little man drinks was like feeding a donkey one oat at a time.

I asked Henri about Arthur and he replied that he knew any amount but could not for the life of him recall anything at such short notice. He was aware that I had made arrangements for a bed at the bistro and by tomorrow he would have probably remembered about Arthur so I was not to worry as he would be staying in the neighbourhood. Now he took my future in hand.

Books about tunny boats and King Arthur, he told me taking another of my cigarettes, were all very well in their way but if I wanted to make my fortune I should write one on the life of his uncle who was also called Henri. I have grown familiar with this line of conversation and said that one day I was going to write a book entitled 'Books That I've Been Given Great Ideas For'. But Henri took no notice, merely remarking that a book on the theme of his Uncle Henri would be a better bet. The conversation continued in this vein and all evening I could see the brown dog scowling through the glass door. The underwear was no longer evident but I made sure he didn't get in.

Henri was still at the table when I bid him goodnight to climb the stairs to my room. The bed was warm from the sun and the sheets smelled faintly of lavender. Despite the rock-filled bolster which serves for a pillow in France I fell asleep to the sound of doves cooing in the eaves.

2 An Old Monk of Great Renown

There were already two people waiting to meet me next morning. One was Henri who had ordered a litre of wine on my account and had kindly tested three-quarters of it to see if it were poisoned. And the other, as the *madame* told me in a hushed voice as she shepherded me down the stairs, was *un policier*.

The French seem keen on guying themselves. Chefs dress the part in tall white hats, thin pencil moustaches and appear with a wine bottle dangling between thumb and forefinger. Butchers wear striped aprons and white forage caps, bakers are covered with flour, ladies' underwear salesmen affect sharp suits and lead shoddy sex lives — and the gendarme pacing up and down in the bar looked everything I had come to expect from French farce.

Portly, with a droopy moustache, with a gun belt supporting his belly, despite the early hour he wore sunglasses. He chewed a cigarette with the corner of his mouth. He was officious but polite and examined my identity card through clouds of smoke. His voice was like a gravel path.

He had come, he informed me, to investigate a complaint made to him by a Madame Cleverdick or some such name. In Brittany family names invariably end with 'ic' or 'ec' which like 'mac' in Scotland means 'the children of'. Was I, he wanted to know, the owner of one large brown dog? I might have guessed it.

I protested that I was not the owner, that I hated the dog, and never wanted to see it again. The gendarme jotted my reply in his notebook with much sucking of teeth. He wanted to see my identity card again and looked from the photograph to me several times to see if he could pierce my clever disguise while he thought of his next move. He now wanted to put the question another way. Was I at the time of the alleged theft *in charge* of the dog? I replied that I certainly was not.

But did I know the dog in question? I had to admit that I did. The gendarme thought that amounted to the same thing. Henri who had been listening intently nodded his head vigorously in support of the official view. Things looked bad but surprisingly the gendarme snapped his notebook shut and said that he was satisfied but on one condition. He had my dog outside in his *camionette* and if I undertook to remove it from his jurisdiction all would be well. I would of course have to pay for the knickers but as they were worn perhaps two francs would cover the damage.

I said I was grateful but although I loved animals dearly I was walking through Brittany and the dog might deter inn and lodging house keepers. The gendarme took out his notebook again and asked to see my identity card. This might have gone on indefinitely if Henri hadn't gallantly offered to remove the dog from the district for me. He did add that we were going in the same direction and would arrange matters later. This was news to me, particularly as I had not told Henri which way I was going. But I paid the two francs, thankful the gendarme had not decided to hold me pending further enquiries.

The gendarme saluted and went out to his van to release the brute which bounded into the bistro like a bundle of springs and into Henri's lap. Only the knickers which he had retrieved from somewhere prevented him from licking the little man's face. Henri produced a length of rope from his pocket already spliced into loops at both ends which served admirably for a lead. He slipped it round the dog's neck.

'*Gespeoc'h, ki,*' he ordered and the dog dived under the table and lay still. This 'keep quiet, dog' in Breton so readily obeyed rang a loud alarm bell in my brain but I decided not to press the issue at that moment. The gendarme did not seem to be suspicious for he left without further comment after wishing us all a pleasant journey.

I needed to travel far to the north and west to Dubglas, but first wanted to visit Saint Gildas's hermitage near Bieuzy on the River Blavet. My most pleasant route, avoiding towns and major roads, would be through the forested region known as the Landes de Lanvaux. Ideally my starting point was near the small village of Saint Guyomard. I proposed to take a hire car there, giving me a walk of twenty-six kilometres to Locmine, not too ambitious for a first day, taking me about half way to Bieuzy. Failing this I could turn off short out of the forest and put up for the night at Saint Jean Brévelay.

Henri was clearly alarmed by my plan, broadly hinting that the Landes were like the Matto Grosso and attempting to walk through them on my own was inviting disaster. Anyway he had a bad leg and he had *my* dog to consider which hated trees. Somehow he would get a lift to Saint Jean and meet me in the evening, 'if I ever arrived at all' he added, shaking his mournful jowls. I liked this idea for Henri seemed to be intent on forming a permanent attachment, me being the provider. I wanted to travel alone. I ordered a hot *croissant* and a bowl of coffee and milk while Henri fortified himself by finishing the litre.

Henri said 'by the way' he had remembered a legend to do with King Arthur if I cared to hear it. This was hopeful and I responded to his unspoken request for a glass of wine to grease the wheels of the story. He hadn't a memory for names but one was called Mark. I was fascinated but not wanting to prompt him remained silent. Henri was wearing the Breton cunning look but I thought this might be due to prolonging the story so that more wine would be needed. He recounted it slowly, stuttering more than usual. According to Henri a man went to Ireland to bring back a wife.

'Who, Mark?' I asked.

'No, no, another. I can't think of his name.'

'Go on,' I pressed him.

Henri told me that in Ireland this other man and Mark's future wife had drunk a love potion intended for the nuptials and had consequently fallen so deeply in love they would never be able to leave off. They had fled to a great forest and lived there for a long time. But Mark hunted them night and day and eventually they were captured. Mark agreed to spare their lives, for he was very angry, if the man would leave Brittany and never return. What could they do? Their tears fell like rain and all the animals and birds of the forest wept with them.

Many years later the exiled one had been wounded by a poisoned arrow and was near death and only true love could save him. So he sent for the one he had loved all his life, telling her to come in a ship with a white sail. If she no longer loved him she was to send a ship with a black sail. But this man's wife had tricked him for in the meantime he had married another and she was jealous. She told him that a ship with a black sail was closing the land. So he died of a broken heart, and so did Mark's widow for the ship had a white sail and she was coming to be with him forever.

I thought a lot about Henri's tale during the car journey to Saint Guyomard. It was none other than the tragic love story of *Tristram and Iseult*, reckoned to be far older than Chrétien de Troyes but later adopted into the Arthurian cycle when he had made Tristram one of Arthur's knights. The 'Mark' was King Mark of Cornwall. Richard Wagner had used the theme for his epic opera *Tristan und Isolde*.

But I was beginning to wonder about Henri. Why had he told me a story about King Mark which was obviously a confection of the French romancers? If he were at all attuned to the subject he would instead have told me a legend told in the area of Brittany where we both came from, which was less formal but as pure Celt as whisky.

Not far from my village is the peninsula called Penmarc'h which forms the lower arm of the Baie d'Audierne. The headland must have had great significance for the pre-Christian religion we call Druidism as the entire area is rich in standing stones and old graves.

The Christians were clearly worried about the atmosphere of Penmarc'h for they took a great deal of trouble to attack the stones, either by pulling them down or resculpturing them to resemble crude crucifixes. But the work must have proved too arduous for later the monks and priests contented themselves with cementing small crosses to the summits of the stones. This desecration was called 'Christianizing'.

Oddly enough, this had only proved the power of the older religion. The so-called 'pagan' monoliths have stood firm despite the battering of countless storms. The puny crosses are broken and wearing away. Far more destructive is the modern idea of gathering together the old monuments at a central museum so that they can be marvelled at by tourists without walking too far from their cars.

A local legend says that a great city once stood at Penmarc'h but it was destroyed by the Saxons. The rubble, strangely said to be of red granite for this material is not local, smashed to tiny fragments, is supposed to be around somewhere. I've never seen it and although everyone knows where it is they are unable to take you there. Maybe this is a memory of something now submerged for the great lowering of the sea at the spring and autumn equinoxes reveals more standing stones and passage graves.

Out there amongst the great overfalls that sweep round the headland is the hunting ground of King Mark of Cornwall. When the storms boil off Penmarc'h that is his season. He can be heard in full cry over the waves. His horse has wings and is the kind known in

Breton legend as a '*mormarc'h*'.

One day Mark, or Marc'h as he is called locally, came across a great white deer of wondrous beauty with a gold crown about its neck. He launched an arrow but the deer seemed immortal, the arrow rebounded and killed the '*mormarc'h*'. Mad with rage Mark throws his silver hunting knife. As it enters the breast of the animal it changes into an even more beautiful princess with long golden hair. She is sometimes called Dahud or Ahes, daughter of King Gradlon of Brittany, who courted the Devil and caused his wonderful city of Ys to sink beneath the waves. Other legends say she was Morgane, the voluptuous sister of King Arthur. King Mark is smitten with love and goes hunting no more.

It was past noon when we reached Saint Guyomard but I was determined not to waste another day. I bought half a loaf and some garlic sausage in the village and struck into the forest with no more ado. It was a foolish decision for I was not equipped for any emergency, not that I anticipated one despite Henri's pessimism. I was travelling light carrying only a change of underwear and a spare shirt and sweater in a small canvas haversack. I did have a lightweight waterproof anorak but I certainly was not equipped for a night in the open at that time of the year. And already I could feel flecks of rain on my face. Rain would considerably hamper my progress.

I was thinking more of my feet. I loved my old walking shoes but for no other reason than they had been with me a long time. They were built in an era which believed in durability and were of tough hide with stiff unpliant soles. Something has to give and I soon realized when the blisters began to explode on my heels and toes that it would be my feet.

I had countless arguments about those shoes and defended them like old friends and just as pointlessly. I had argued my way one hundred and fifty kilometres or so across the old Neolithic highway along the chalk downs of Sussex and Hampshire. I had on occasion resorted to stockinged feet to ease the pain but still held that they were the finest walking shoes in the world. In fact they were the worst.

The forest floor was uneven and studded with flints and I can thoroughly recommend the experience to anyone wishing to take up fire walking. I found myself constantly kicking my ankles but what caused this phenomenon I cannot explain. The forest was mostly conifers with the odd oak and beech but the rides were badly overgrown with brambles like barbed wire, and soon these old paths faded out entirely. To ease the burden I dropped down toward the southern skirt of the trees which helped but I was now heading in the wrong direction. The light began to fade as the once clear sky changed to a white, opaque ceiling. The wind gusted in the higher branches and the birds fell silent, presaging a deterioration in the weather.

At one time the Landes were a refuge for the great Breton resistance to the forces of the Revolution. Brittany was still Royalist long after the rest of France had succumbed to the Terror. During the recent war the Landes were the haunt of the Resistance and the occupying Germans expended much time and energy trying to winkle them out. They were never entirely successful.

Even today, as I found to the cost of my skin, the forest is largely inpenetrable. One of the difficulties of traversing the Landes is the large number of water-filled gulleys which run down from the higher ground and at right angles to the lines of trees, and to my route. This meant much retracing of steps, and death defying leaps. The landing platforms seemed to have been prepared by some practical joker with thick beads of brambles and thistles.

There is much to remind you of the Druids in the Landes who preferred woodland glades to worshipping their deities. I was frequently coming across standing stones, majestic in their isolation, and 'dolmens', so called because the large flat stones of which they are formed resemble something like a gigantic stone table. The name comes from two Breton words for 'table' and 'stone' — 'taol' and 'men' but I've been told that 'taol' might have been 'daol' which means 'devil' for tradition holds them as the homes of evil spirits.

I stumbled into two frightening standing stones or rather one had fallen over or had been pushed. The tops of the pillars had been carved into grotesque parodies of human heads. These, I learned later were known locally as 'Monsieur and Madame Baboon'. They are not nice to look at and these combining with the jumping and frustration had me badly rattled. I began to worry about the significance of these sculptures and my thoughts were full of human sacrifices and blood letting in general. I found myself hurrying and I was happy when I struck a small rough path leading off somewhere to my right. Only a triumph of folly made me cross and continue into the trees beyond. It was now raining heavily.

I reckoned I had come about six kilometres since entering the forest and identified the track as one on my map which was just half way to Saint Jean Brévelay. I thought I had at least another three hours of daylight. This was a miscalculation because my watch had stopped at one of the water jumps. Another two hours of thrashing through underbrush with the daylight almost gone showed me my error.

The treetops had by now become loaded with all the rain they could hold and were pouring it down my neck. The earth underfoot was a slippery paste. It was so dark now I could not see my small pocket compass and floundering about in the forest all night would be inviting a broken leg. I could no longer escape the obvious, I would have to pass the night in the haunted forest. My lodging was, horribly, one of the dolmens.

The grave made quite an efficient shelter. There were plenty of old sticks, probably blown into the hole during the previous autumn. I managed to light a small fire with my last match and some dead leaves. This made a lot of smoke and some heat but my clothes were soaked and all night I steamed gently. I was grateful to my host who probably died about five thousand years ago but the place was full of ghosts.

For all my years in Brittany I knew the interior very little and it was a different kind of quiet. I missed the sound of the sea. Alone in the flickering shadows of my fire I could not keep my mind off the *ankou*. It is said by strangers that the Bretons seem more than usually preoccupied by death. I often argued that maybe their cheerful fatalistic attitude in fact might be a preoccupation with life, but perhaps I'm wrong.

The terror of old people in rural areas in Brittany is the *ankou*. He is a human skeleton in a dark robe and when your time is nigh he comes to fetch you in his *karrig*, a dark coach drawn by darker horses. He is also spoken of as '*Gwilherm koz*' or 'Old Bill' but this is when the lights are bright and there is company, never in an isolated dolmen at midnight. On the coast the *ankou's* funerary coach is replaced by a *bag noz* — the 'boat of the night'. The figure at the helm of this terrible vessel, if you are unfortunate enough to see her, is the first to die the next year. It is usually you.

But to my mind the most frightening Breton belief about the dead coming to fetch the living are the '*kannerezed koz*' — 'the old washer-women'. You might see some old ladies round the kind of open air washing places where I had first seen Madame Cleverdick. These communal *lavoirs* are common throughout rural France, large stone pools fed by a natural spring.

The old ladies beckon you over and you go because you think you know them. And you do for they are the dead of the village. Then they hand you your shroud. So great is the fear of the washers that the men of my village keep clear of the *lavoir* even in broad daylight. A short cut from the quay to my cottage passes such a *lavoir*. Petit Jean who I had worked with on a small crab boat was most alarmed when he saw my intention of taking the small path late one evening. Then after much hesitation he told me about the *kannerezed koz*. But our owner and despot Josée Priol did tell me that Jean's reluctance was more likely due to the fact that Tante'phine's lay by the longer route.

To drag my mind away from the *ankou* I made myself think of something jolly, and it seems the jolliest topic I could manage at the time was those rollicking rapists, Arthur's enemies, the Saxons. Historians seem to imagine that the Saxons were capable of rowing across vast stretches of sea then coming running ashore to rape and pillage. From my experience of the sea I cannot find this at all plausible. Maybe my saturated night in the dolmen brought this home to me more forcefully. Even a short sea voyage is exhausting and the attackers would be in no condition for such junketing.

It seems more likely that our Saxons on sighting some suitable target would land further up the coast to rest up a little, then work their way inland to attack from that side so as to stop the defenders escaping with the loot. From Nennius one gathers that quite a number of attractive settlements lay up rivers. The Saxons, excellent seamen that they were, would know how to work the tides so as to hit hard and fast before a defence could be organized. It would be no use slogging away against the ebb tide. Nor would they come roaring up the river on the full flood. Slack water and the beginning of the ebb would be the ideal time for the attack.

Much has been written about the bloody temperament of these Scandinavian warriors of the early centuries of this era, of their ghastly lust for the destruction and slaughter even at the expense of gain. Saint Gildas, who never pulled a metaphor when it came to describing enemies, (and it seems he had few friends) is very descriptive about Saxon methods:

'Every colony is levelled to the ground by the stroke of the battering ram. The inhabitants are slaughtered along with the guardians of their churches, priests and people alike, while the sword gleamed on every side, and the flames crackled around. How horrible to behold in the midst of the streets the tops of towers torn from their lofty hinges, the stones of high walls, holy altars, mutilated corpses, all covered with lurid clots of coagulated blood, as if they had been crushed together in some ghastly winepress . . . Of the miserable remnant some flee to the hills, only to be captured and slain in heaps; some constrained by famine, come in and surrender themselves to be slaves for ever to the enemy . . . Others wailing bitterly pass overseas.'

It must be remembered that this account was written by a monk who hated the Saxons not only as anti-Christs but for the relentless destruction of his world. Lately there has been a counter-attack by Scandinavian scholars who say that such descriptions are extravagent nonsense and in fact their forebears were creatures of love and light. The truth lies somewhere between these extreme views, and just where is best left for individual conjecture, but 'Saxon' comes from the Nordic word for 'sword' and a gentle people would not be named after a tool for killing.

What would these sea warriors of the sixth century have looked like? Most likely they would have been not too unlike the Vikings of two centuries later of whom we have adequate descriptions. They would be tall, stocky, bearded individuals and it would be best to stand upwind of them. They dressed in a rough woollen jerkin which reached the thighs, tight woollen trousers and leather sandals. They would wear some kind of light leather armour or possibly looted chain mail. Over this would be thrown a loose woollen cloak, secured by a brooch which left the right arm free for butchery. The helmet, a close fitting skull cap, might sometimes have been of iron but more frequently of leather. Whether it had horns on it or not is still the subject of debate but it is thought unlikely. He carried a round wooden shield, perhaps covered with hide, and he would be armed with a short sword, called the 'sahs', maybe a spear and an axe.

There would have been very little difference between the dress of the Saxons and that of Arthur and his men. The only point of contention seems to be whether they would have been equestrians. In one of Caesar's most descriptive passages he spoke of the terror inspired in his men by the Celtic horsemen. He put it down to the unaccustomed sight of masses of horses and the roar of the chariot wheels, sufficient in themselves to throw the opposition into disorder.

The chariots were manned by a driver and a spearman and attacked through squadrons of cavalry. The spearmen dismounted and fought on foot, the charioteers drawing off a little distance but coming thundering back if the spearman became hard pressed. Thus, said Caesar, they combined the mobility of cavalry with the resilience of infantry.

The Romans marvelled that even on a steep incline the charioteers could control their horses at full gallop, checking and turning them instantly. And the skill of the spearmen who could run out along the chariot shaft between the two horses and stand on the yoke, and then nip back into the chariot in an instant also impressed them very much.

Caesar's armies in Gaul boasted cavalry said to be entirely made up of Celtic mercenaries or renegades. An attack by these fierce horsemen was an awesome sight, and as deadly. But Julius never trusted them for being Celts they were likely to turn coat and fight on the other side. They had horse games, which seem to have resembled equestrian rugby football but the idea was to put the head of some luckless adversary over the line. Caesar never says so but through his words comes the impression that his allies were wild maniacs.

The current view is that Arthur would have been a foot soldier although it seems incredible that such skill in martial horsemanship should have been allowed to atrophy. The use of cavalry was the deciding factor in almost every military engagement up until the invention of the machine-gun. It was William's horsemen who won the Battle of Hastings, and Cromwell's cavalry who shattered King Charles's army at Naseby. Much more recently it was the Boer cavalry who held the entire army of the British Empire at bay.

The Welsh certainly used a kind of cavalry. The bane of Edward III was sudden attacks on his supply columns by bands of fierce painted savages who swept down the mountain passes on shaggy ponies, accompanied by great blasts on war horns. Geoffrey of Monmouth put King Arthur on horseback but this is usually explained away by the view that the monk was a noble and he could not conceive of a king being dismounted. Walking was only for serfs and peasants. But the weight of modern scholarship is strong for a marching Arthur. His logistic would have been foot power.

Let us get back to the appearance of our Arthur. Some classical authors say that Celtic warriors wore nothing, that they went into battle carrying only their weapons, an attack, it seems, resembling a fire at a nudist colony. But I'm not going to have this for classical writers were fond of depicting their adversaries as naked savages. Neither can I conceive of Arthur resembling a Saxon. For me he is the more picturesque figure that I met in a book of lithographs.

Arthur's woollen tunic and his cloak would have been woven in a pattern which showed his tribe and his standing as a leader. It would be a plaid, not in the garish colours of modern kilts but more those of the misty moors and the tints of autumn. His broadsword rested in a leather shoulder belt fastened with a buckle bright with a cairngorm. Carried on a similar belt would be his great round shield, a good four feet in diameter. Rather than a boring dome his helmet was a double-decker pot with a great plume of eagle feathers. Belted round his waist and hanging in front would be a leather pouch, a prototype sporran perhaps.

I knew Arthur's face well. He would have a small beard but his features would be dominated by a great drooping moustache. His eyes would be clever and bright like new pennies, his cheeks ruddy, somewhat wasted. In fact the whole would have that noble dissipation one sees on the faces of old Scottish pipers.

I had needed Arthur's shrewdness on the banks of the Glein and courage in the dolmen. He would have been wise like an old Celtic warrior would have had to have been. I had never met a Breton quite like him but somehow he was the epitome of them all. He would be someone I could consult during my journey through his land. He came from the shadows in the dolmen and he wouldn't go away. It seemed about four days later before it was light enough for me to continue my journey. When I broke out of the Landes Arthur was still at my heels. Sometimes I found myself turning to talk to him out loud. He was with me all the way to his death at Camlann.

Saint Jean was no more than a cluster of stone cottages with the inevitable bistro cum grocery store. Inside, almost as inevitably, was Henri with the dog and a partly consumed bottle of wine, the former in no small heat about my tardiness. He said that he had thought of organizing a search party but never quite explained why he had not, except that he had entertained on my behalf the dog and three young musicians who were, he said, desperate to meet me. The group called themselves '*Ar Mor Braz*'.

'The Big Sea' wore a costume I had only seen before in old photographs and at Breton folk festivals and which I had sworn I could not be induced to put on by torture. The hat resembled a wide brimmed flat crowned bowler bedecked by ribbons which hung down the back. A single breasted black velvet jacket was worn over a high necked double breasted waistcoat, plum coloured with small gilt buttons. This is not so bad but the most worrying garment was the large, white, pleated but still voluminous cotton drawers, called '*bragou braz*' meaning the 'big breeches'. These were tucked into white socks and held there with garters with large pom-poms.

This strange costume was still worn in Brittany until well after the Kaiser War and much later by diehards and eccentrics. Youenn, Fanchic and Yann explained that they were on their way to Quimper — Kemper as they insisted on calling it — for the great festival of Cornailles, about one hundred kilometres to the north west. They would be in plenty of time, I thought, for it was not held until the end of July and all of four months hence. But they intended to keep themselves in the meantime by playing at baptisms, weddings and other bibulous occasions to which the Bretons are particularly vulnerable.

Those three young men were of a kind not unusual in Brittany. Through folk music they had been led to Breton 'Nationalism', a movement which only serves the French right. Metropolitan France has always sniffed at the Bretons. If the story of the Breton migration was to be believed then the Bretons were interlopers and should behave like guests in a foreign land. But the Bretons had not behaved and they resisted all attempts to absorb them into the French nation.

Brittany has been officially French for over four hundred years, since Anne de Bretagne married the king of France, but the duchess's subjects have behaved as if they had not been invited to the wedding. The phrase 'with the exception of Brittany' pulses through French history like the harmony of a Bach fugue and exemplifies the sometimes bitter struggle between French arrogance and Breton cussedness. Sheer muscle power failing the French tried a more subtle form of combat at which the parent nation excelled — bureaucracy. This manifested itself in a kind of cultural genocide, the active discouragement of Breton place names, the total banning of the Breton language in schools, and of Breton names at christenings.

Old Fayot had told me of the agony of a small child being taught the 'three Rs' in a language of which he could make very little. He had grown to love the French language as much as the methods used to implant it. The children were sent to cut the teaching aids themselves. The withies were used by their fathers to construct and repair crab and lobster pots and their fathers showed them how old withies neither hurt much nor stood much striking against a little boy's backside. The thrashings were marked with mock cries of pain and the flying debris of the fragile birches. The French schoolmasters used to wonder why pots made of such frail material could survive a storm while Breton schoolmasters guessed the truth but said nothing.

This was the reason why 'The Big Sea' insisted on calling themselves Youenn, Fanchic, and Yann instead of Yvon, François and Jean, and Kemper instead of Quimper. Other manifestations of this Nationalism are the alteration of road signs into Breton and aerosol slogans in Breton on public walls telling the French to go back to France which the French can make little of. More serious of late and with increasing frequency are the bombings of public works deemed offensive to Breton sensibilities, including the destruction of a television mast because the local station's programmes were too French in content. Sadly this deprived older Bretons of their only source of entertainment for the two months it took to repair.

Much to the annoyance of the *madame*, my baggy-trousered acquaintances decided to stir up the dust of the bistro with an impromptu concert. Breton airs are an acquired taste which the instruments do little to foster. Of Breton bagpipes little good can be said. They squeal and the first few notes cause the teeth to clench and eyes to water. The call of its playmate, the *'bombarde'*, is like a reedy trumpet and remarkably similar to the nasal piping of mating herring gulls. Percussion is supplied by pounding a small side drum and the rhythmic clogging of the other members of the *begad* as the trio is called. After a few preliminary brays, twitters and thumps and a cry of alarm from the *madame*, the *begad* struck up with '*Ar Dri Mataloen*' with shocking imprecision and volume.

Henri, excited by the wine and music, hauled me to my feet and we went into the sideways shuffle and hop of 'The Three Sailors', according to the lyrics drunk, to which my fatigue from the night in the dolmen and my blisters lent terrible realism. But the movement did have the effect of ridding my clothes and shoes of some of the mud with which they were caked.

After an hour or so, it seemed, the song and we were exhausted and we sat down and called for more wine which the *madame* refused to serve until 'The Big Sea' promised there would be no repetition of the cabaret. Temporarily frustrated, Youenn told me that the three of them had been at the Fish School at Lorient but had decided that fishing was only fit for peasants and they had forsaken all for folk music.

I rejoindered that I thought that folk music had been invented by peasants but the subtlety of the humour was lost on the musicians and they became angry, then apologized, ordering more wine to make up. They said that I ought to forget about King Arthur and write a book about Breton folk music which would make my fortune.

Henri could not agree and still thought that Uncle Henri would prove the better moneyspinner. If I was intent on folly, however, he had remembered another legend to do with King Arthur. This time he told me about Sir Yvain who had found an enchanted fountain in a forest with a fierce guardian who he had fought and slain, but not before he had inflamed the Black Knight by pouring some magic water from the spring on a stone which had unleashed a storm. The victorious Yvain had done the decent thing by marrying the Black Knight's beautiful widow. Henri had gained the impression that Yvain had a pet lion but he could not remember the details, and anyway I had been given enough to be going on with.

I had. I was now convinced that Henri's half-recollected legends were being mugged up. The story of Sir Yvain, also called the Knight of the Lion, was pure Chrétien de Troyes. At this juncture Youenn decided that a promise extracted under duress was no promise at all and nothing would serve but a loud blast of '*Ar Pont Callec*'. The old lady did not agree. She was entirely indifferent to 'The Wooden Bridge' and made a dart for the telephone, swearing she would summon the *gendarmerie*. I led the dash out into the sunlight.

Locmine was only ten kilometres or two hours' march up the road but it seemed to last an eternity. As a matter of honour no bistro could be passed and I was too weak to protest. We must have presented a strange sight. My feet were so sore I had removed my shoes and hung them from my neck by the laces. The road was rough but walking in stockinged feet was sheer bliss. Ahead of us trotted our mascot with the knickers, now rent into a nightmare.

All the time Henri was stuttering his protests at my insinuation that he must have read the Arthurian legends somewhere. He shouted loudly that contrary proof was that he had now recollected the name of the forest which was called Brocelien and that was a real forest near Paimpont. If Brocelien was a real place what did I mean

by suggesting that he had read about Tristram and thingummybob
and Yvain the Lion? Behind us came the *begad* in full wail about '*The
Virgins of Camaret*' and how they were responsible for the shortage.

I stopped to ask an elderly woman if we were right for Locmine.
After examining us with sad eyes to my intense surprise she shrieked
with laughter then ran indoors. This foxed me completely until I
found out that Saint Columban of Locmine was the patron saint of
idiots.

The wine and the hot sun took its toll. Henri fell into the hedge and
refused to move. *Ar Mor Vraz* decided loyally to stay with him and
sat down nearby tooting and thumping their instruments. Sticking
out of Henri's pocket was a small volume. I took it out and the cover
told me it was the *Petite Encyclopédie de Litérature Française*. On
page fifteen were the potted legends of Tristram and Yvain. This was
Henri's crib. In disgust I decided to continue my journey alone. My
last view of Henri, at least at the time I thought it was, was a pair of
rubber boots which appeared to be stuttering: '*We will meet at Paimpont.*'

To me this sounded like Antony's threat to Brutus about meeting
at Philippi. The dreadful dog trotted after me for a few paces but
then dashed back to Henri's leafy bower. If the little man had not
been the owner before he was now.

If you look like a tramp never try a third rate hotel in the hope that
you will resemble the other lodgers so much that your scruffiness will
not be objected to. Small hotels are as particular about their reputa-
tions as unemployed politicians and you will be told to return to your
swamp. First rate hotels do not have to be as careful and more likely
you will be suspected of being an eccentric millionaire and treated
kindly. So it was at Locmine. The receptionist stuck plasters on my
feet and took my clothes for cleaning while I recovered in bed. The
owner's wife drove me on to Bieuzy the next morning.

There are more small Breton towns like Bieuzy than not. When the
countryside needed a large population of agricultural workers
Bieuzy was important but now the town seems to exist for no reason
at all, like an unwanted woman. The buildings are very old, the granite carved with a delicacy that the world no longer cares about, old
stone turned brown with ages of weathering, mottled with lichen of
light green turning to startling gold.

Nearby are the remains of the great abbey of Castennec, so ruined
as to be not worth the trouble of a visit. Tradition says that here lived

the exiled British monk Saint Gildas or to use the Celtic form of this cantankerous man's came — Gweltas. The town is named for his devoted companion and disciple, Bieuzy. He seems to have been leader of the community, that is when he wasn't running errands for snappy old Gildas.

When we hear the term 'monk' we think of the Roman Catholic kind but Celtic monks were quite different in appearance. Gildas would have worn a long woollen robe which was roughly similar to the Vatican habit but it would have been coarsely woven and the dirty yellow of fleece. Accounts mention a working apron or jerkin of leather worn over the top. But the striking difference would have been in the tonsure, not the neat shaven crown but shaved from ear to ear given the high forehead considered to be the mark of intellectuality. Otherwise the hair was left uncut, falling to the shoulders.

This hair style inflamed Rome, so much so that it caused a major rift between the Celtic monks of Britain and those of Saint Peter. But the two kinds never got on. It seemed to Rome that the Celts had invented a religion of their own. They insisted on celebrating important events in the religious calendar on different dates to those ordained by the pope, causing an alarming state of affairs where one community would be fasting while another feasted.

It was Rome, however, that was always tinkering with the calendar. The Celts stuck doggedly to dates which had some bearing on agriculture as indicated by the phases of the moon and the rotation of the stars in the heavens, not dates produced by the whim of some pope thousands of miles away at Rome.

So a peculiar religious war developed with rival communities of monks competing for business against their neighbours. The Celts were forever breaking new ground, making new converts, only to be followed by Pope Gregory's monks with their new ideas and calendar.

Miracles are no longer the fashion and one wonders whether the temperature of Heaven's interest in us has cooled or if the monks who popped miracles into their writing as easily as punctuation were just plain crazy. But the monks did use one of the most powerful hallucigens known to man. It was called starvation. Most of them never ate flesh, seldom fish, but made do with bells and lengthy readings from the gospel, keeping alive with a little honey and milk.

Gildas seems to have been on a diet for he ate and drank neither, and according to one biographer sat in icy cold rivers instead. In addition to the traditional methods used by the monks to improve the soul by mortifying the flesh such as kneeling on sharp stones and flagellation, Gildas wore a hair shirt stuck full of needles. But it must be remembered that these may have been of bone and not steel so not as excruciating as it sounds.

Gildas is supposed to have been born in Scotland at Arecluta or Arclwd, now Dumbarton, just after the year A.D. 500. He is said to have been of noble blood, even a prince, and one of a very large family of sons and daughters who, the hagiographers write hopefully, gave their fortunes to the Church and became monks and nuns. One exception was a savage brother who was little thought of. One account surprisingly says that this brother was slain by King Arthur and that it was through spite that Gildas did not name him as the victor of Mount Badon.

Gildas learned to read and write under the tutelage of a hermit of a small island off the area where Barrow-in-Furness now stands. He served his novitiate at the monastery of Sain Iltud, in South Wales who survives today in the scarcely edifying place name Llantwit. Then he travelled to Brittany, to solitary exile on the lonely island of Houst in the Morbihan. Later he built a monastery on the mainland at the invitation of the local chieftain, Warok. Then Gildas travelled everywhere as a missionary, first to Rome where he slew a dragon and defeated brigands who attempted to rob him by paralysing them with prayer, back to Britain, then Ireland and Scotland. Then he returned to Brittany.

That Gildas wrote his famous history which he frankly calls his 'complaining book' in Brittany is either unknown or ignored by historians preferring to find Mount Badon in Britain. This point is made unsensationally by a monk while intending to praise Gildas for troubling himself to write up the stories of dispossessed monks. The actual passage runs:

'Once more the holy man, at the request of brother monks who came to him from Britain, ten years after he had departed from the country, wrote a short epistolary book in which he reproved five kings of that island who had been ensnared by various crimes. He elegantly and concisely related their wickedness.'

Some authorities have complicated the issue with the 'duplication' theory, a clever device which allows you to accuse another authority of lying without actually calling him a liar. This says that there must have been two Saints Gildas, one born about A.D. 425 in Brittany, possibly a contemporary of King Arthur, and another born about a hundred years later in Britain who wrote the 'complaining book'. Even a three Saints Gildas theory has been advanced.

But all this ignores the monk's simple statement that the only Saint Gildas he knew came from Britain and wrote the book in Brittany. And if there were two Saints Gildas then Rome doesn't know about the other one. A letter from the Abbot of Luxeuil to Pope Gregory, written sometime between A.D. 595 and A.D. 600 makes no distinction and this was only 175 years away from the birth of the supposedly earlier Saint Gildas and within a few years of the death of the other. Even the cautious monk Bede, who quoted Gildas at length, knows no other monk of the same name. For me Gildas wrote *De Excidio et Conquestu Britanniae* on the banks of the Blavet.

Gildas was always mad at dragons. One lived in a hole at Ponvin near his monastery on the shore of the Morbihan. Its breath was so foul it caused plague and it was necessary to placate the beast once a year with a human sacrifice. Taking off his hair shirt Gildas fed it to the brute and the needles trapped him like fish hooks. Towing the dragon with the hair shirt as a lead Gildas mounted his winged horse and flew out over the Morbihan where he cut the shirt and the dragon fell into the sea and drowned.

This monkish preoccupation with dragon slaying seems childish to us but it is likely that the monks were not really writing about a fierce beast at all, that the dragon was allegory for something more deadly for the Christian religion. This legend of Saint Gildas gives us a clue as to what this was. The time for the annual human sacrifice to the Penvin dragon is given as All Souls' Day. This was also the commencement of the Druid Feast of Samain, known for hideous and terrifying rites, such as human sacrifices with burnings of the victims in huge wicker cages. There can't be much doubt then that what the monks referred to as dragons, imps, demons, and Satan, were Gildas's spiritual competitors — the Druids. Gildas was not fighting dragons but competing for congregations.

The church at Bieuzy is like most French churches, barren and disappointing. In addition to the ears, noses and sexual organs of the effigies of the nobility which for some reason seem to have offended the Revolution, the *sans-culottes* also ran off with all the old furnishings, the only two objects of interest being a rock which sounds something like a gong when struck with a hammer stone, and a painting on wood showing the soul of Bieuzy's murderer in torment. This was the monk's sad end.

As Gildas's friend was saying Mass he was interrupted by a messenger from the local chief who wanted to go hunting but all his hounds had annoyingly developed rabies during the night. What was needed was a quick miracle so as not to spoil the day's sport. Bieuzy reminded the messenger that it was the Sabbath and told him that the miracle would have to wait till Monday. The reward for this devotion came swiftly for shortly the chief himself appeared to bury a hunting knife in poor Bieuzy's head.

Gildas was away at his monastery by the sea shore and Bieuzy walked the eighty kilometres with the hunting knife sticking out of his head, no doubt looking like a trolleycar. Waiting to carry him across the Morbihan was a white boat manned by oarsmen dressed in white. Gildas pulled out the knife but the monk died in his arms. The revengeful saint goes to the chief and curses him with the result that his hounds chew him to pieces.

It was raining quite hard as I left the town and walked the two kilometres to the Blavet. Breton rivers are still wooded and beautiful, untouched by the curse of 'nature trails', and apart from the French habit of corsetting them into canals as they pass through towns they are mostly unspoiled. They also have delicious sounding names like Brandifrute and some have names that you seem to have heard before like Odet, Canut, Claie and Oust. The Blavet is no exception and just above Bieuzy is straight and about twenty metres from bank to bank, lined with beech, ash and oak. By the time I reached Gildas's cell the rain was bouncing high off the surface of the river. A small stream pursued me down the steep, narrow path.

This is not Gildas's original cell and it doesn't look as medieval as the guide books say it is. But the shade of the saint is there all right. We have a brief glimpse of the monk at the time he wrote his 'complaining book'. It is not a contemporary account by a few hundred years but its personal description must be unique for the early chroniclers dwelt on the sanctity of the saint's soul not the size of his boots.

According to this informative scribe Gildas was very tall and virtually fleshless and his face was highly coloured, crimson like a man in high fever. After sitting in the cold river until he had said the Lord's Prayer three times Gildas spent the rest of the night naked on a stone bench. He normally wore a goatskin and like the rest of the Scottish nation had an aversion to washing, adds the monk tartly. So cheeky was this remark one wonders if the monk was working out his notice.

The cell was divided into two compartments, an antechamber which was entirely bare except for a long bench, and a small chapel with a stained glass window of about the early nineteenth century and a small altar. There is another stone gong used, says tradition, to summon Bieuzy from the monastery at Castennec.

I sat on the bench and listened to the roar of the rain. The cell is built into a great outcrop of granite some fifty metres in height which shoots the rain down on the slate roof with a force that makes the structure tremble. On this height lived one of Gildas's dragons.

Today the rock is called 'the mountain of Castennec' but it was known as Castle Noë in the Middle Ages and for the Romans it was the fort and 'city' of Sulim. It was named for the goddess, Sul, of whom little is known except that she was worshipped both by the Celts and the occupying Roman troops. The locals know Sul as *'ar Gwreg houarn'* meaning 'the fire maiden' which as a demonstration of efficacy of Breton memory cannot be beaten for one of the trappings of the cult was a perpetual flame.

There used to be two standing stones on the mount but they were pulled down and broken up by the Christian vandals of the last century. They would have been there when Gildas was writing of his countrymen in his book that they were more interested in growing hair on their bodies than covering them with clothes to hide their shameful nakedness.

I had a quick look outside the cell and the sky was a mosaic of black and white cotton wool and if anything the rain appeared to be increasing in volume. The stream was now flooding across the door sill into the cell. But I made the extravagant decision to climb up to the mount before it grew too dark and put on my anorak. I can't explain what happened next. Scrambling over the edge of the rock I received a gigantic push in the chest which sent me skidding down the slope on my back. It could have been a cow but I don't know for I saw nothing. The only likely explanation is that it was one of Arthur's strange troupe of experts and this one's name was Shover. I beat a retreat.

Once more soaked and coated with mud I spent the night as guest of Saint Gildas, on the bench in the antechamber. I'm not sure whether I preferred the dolmen as an ambiance for fear. In the muddy lake under the bench I found a small wooden cross which I placed near my head to ward off the powers of darkness. The morning light revealed the 'cross' to be a child's broken model aeroplane. Anyway it worked. Apart from some nightjars prattling in the drenched trees I passed a wakeful but unhaunted night.

As I climbed up the track from the cell the next morning I could sense I was being followed. It would have been difficult to leave the crusty old gentleman at the Blavet for he is everywhere in Brittany. So supporting himself on a staff — the great crosier with which he is normally depicted being out of place for such a journey — old Gildas of the bloodshot countenance joined Arthur in my select band of travelling companions. It was good to have him along. Not only a fellow countryman, he would be an authority on religious as opposed to military matters. And although I had complete faith in Arthur's slashing Caliburn and darting Ron we might meet with a dragon or two.

3 To the Valley of No Return

As I ate breakfast at the first café in Bieuzy that was not ashamed to have me — a coat of mud now seemed a normal part of my costume — I changed my plans. Henri's parting shot that Brocelien was the old name for the forest at Paimpont was correct I had found. Folded in my notebook was one of my disreputable sources, the picture post-card reproduction of a *circa* sixteenth-century map of Brittany. Instead of Paimpont stood the name 'Brekilien'. Further confirmation of this chance discovery came from a closer look at my Michelin map which had the Frenchified version of the 'Broceliande' for a small village in the heart of the forest.

Chrétien de Troyes had used 'Brocelien' as the playground for his romances. But was the association a chance one? Had Chrétien chosen the forest just because it was the great central forest of Brittany where at one time only the brave would enter? Or had he a better reason? Was it indeed the centre of the Arthurian tradition?

My modern map revealed another startling place name. This time it was the 'Fountain of Barenton'. Barenton was the fountain or spring guarded by the fairy Viviane, where Arthur's baptiser and mentor, the knight and sorceror Merlin was worsted in a rubber of magic and as forfeit was imprisoned forever in a Castle of Air. Wace the Norman had certainly visited Barenton but one doesn't know what to make of his comment which was poetic and obscure.

'I was foolish to go there, and even more foolish to return,' he complained.

It was too tempting. I would have to join Wace in his folly.

But how was I going to get to Paimpont? Another point I had mentally discussed was how much walking and how much riding I would do during my journey around Brittany. At first I was all for walking the entire distance for this way I would have plenty of time to think about all that I had learned about the Bretons and what I was learning. But the Nennius battlefields alone, taken in the correct order, would have me walking nearly nine hundred miles, Arthur's walking of a lifetime. And the Landes had proved that I was no John Hillaby. So I decided to walk or ride as the mood took me. Boring and lengthy hikes along main roads were not for me. They shatter the nerves and destroyed the fragile quality of Celtic Brittany that I was after. After all, even during what he insisted was a pilgrimage on foot Hilaire Belloc cadged lifts from carters on his way to Rome. Why shouldn't I?

My journey to Josselin and over halfway to Paimpont, about eighty kilometres further east, was effected by one of those almost incredible acts of generosity of which the Bretons are capable. The railroad from the nearest large town of Pontivy insisted on going north and west and was no use to me. The round and jovial *patron* of the café shook his head when I enquired about bus connections, implying that such a journey would be beyond man's natural span. Anyway such bother was unnecessary, he casually informed me, as by chance he was going to Josselin that very morning. The cost of such an idea terrified me and seemed set fair to put me in reach of the *assistance publiques* but the *patron* flapped his hands at the mention of payment. Did he not have a sister at Josselin whom he had not seen for years?

The narrow road to Josselin wound through wide almost treeless valleys with tiny, isolated granite farmsteads and the occasional hamlet. Motoring in Brittany out of the tourist season must be very much like pre-war Britain. But the Bretons can give you the impression of post-war Piccadilly with their cut and thrust driving. Yves Jaffrey was a good driver but he must overtake and hated to be overtaken — and he drove using the Breton single finger technique with the air of relaxing in a deckchair.

Jaffrey used to be a miller but he burnt his mill down. Millers were always burning their mills down. It was an occupational hazard like bullfighters being gored by bulls and hardly worth commenting on. The reason lay in the simple fact that you can't reef the sails of a windmill nor turn the tap on a gale by remote control. Nor it might be added, although Yves did not bother to stress the point, can you stop millers going down to the bistro while a batch of corn was being ground. According to Yves you fill up the corn hopper, go down to the bistro, the wind starts to blow a gale, all the corn is ground to flour, the mill stones begin to grind each other, and the sparks ignite the windmill. You get back breathless just in time to stamp out the last embers. It had happened not once but twice to Yves, and Madame Jaffrey, fearing for the little Jaffreys had bought the bistro where neglected wine bottles seldom combust of their own accord. Now everybody was content.

The pink turreted château of Josselin comes on you as a pleasant shock. Sheltering in the wide sweep of a green valley, defended from the front by the wide Oust canal, the medieval town breaks on you suddenly after taking a sharp hill bend. We rushed down on it as if prepared to take the place by storm. Yves would have made an excellent dive bomber pilot.

'Ever been involved with a Josselin woman?' asked the ex-miller, unconcerned by what seemed like our imminent deaths. He said he would not recommend the experience. They had tongues which took flesh from the ears. Evidently it was all to do with a curse laid on the women of the town by a poor female beggar who had asked for a drink of water but had been refused. Instead they'd set the dogs on her. Unfortunately the beggar was in reality the mother of Jesus Christ, the Virgin Mary. As punishment the wives of Josselin were condemned to sound like fighting dogs for perpetuity. I had heard from Fayot that the entire population of Morbihan was known as the 'Ki-kis' because of the strange sound they made when speaking. Oddly enough the people of Finistère are known as the 'Oof-oofs' for the same reason.

According to Yves the Virgin Mary was always turning up in Brittany. In fact if your car broke down it was hardly necessary to phone a garage as the mother of Jesus would be sure to be passing shortly.

'That's if you believe the Christians,' said Yves waspishly. I hoped old Gildas in the back seat had not heard him.

The ex-miller refused my offer of a lunch and having forgotten about his 'sister' he now remembered a pressing engagement back at Locmine. Instead he accepted a glass of wine. Then he shook my hand and promised that I would have more than enough of King Arthur before I left Paimpont.

'Just follow the signposts,' he said on parting.

'To Paimpont?' I asked him curiously.

'No, to King Arthur. You can't avoid him,' he replied. 'Start at Trehorenteuc.' Then he drove off leaving me wondering exactly what he meant.

The village of Trehorenteuc I found from my map was about

twenty-eight kilometres distant, about five hours' steady walking. But not in my present shoes and I resolved to do something about that straight away.

Josselin is a small prim castle town where all the shops stand shoulder to shoulder as if they too were part of the military defences. The stores seem to have done well out of the tourists drawn to the town by the castle and all of them have expensive frontages but the refurbishing has been done with a taste which is far from offensive. The glitter of tourism has been kept to a minimum and nothing like some other Breton resorts where you can't buy a pair of shoelaces which do not have some happy catch phrase on them.

Comfort was to be preferred to style and apart from carpet slippers, to my mind the most comfortable kind of footwear are lightweight canvas tennis shoes, sometimes called sneakers, sometimes deckshoes. I did not invent the idea for Hillaby strode around Africa in them without discomfort.

The only trouble was I did not know the French expression for canvas shoes, a fact I failed to realize before my confrontation in a superior shoe store with a smartly dressed burgher, who seemed to value me at a glance and ring up zero on his mental cash register. After listening to my needs carefully he produced a pair of ski boots, not bad for a part of the world which has never seen snow. I shook my head and explained that the kind I had in mind had canvas uppers and rubber soles. If you could fault my description it was because I erroneously thought that 'canvas' was an international word and used 'cacahouète' for rubber when it in fact means 'peanut'. The word I was looking for was 'caoutchouc'.

The proprietor wearily glanced at his watch and said he was closing while edging me towards the door. It was sheer genius which gave me the idea of running up and down and crying 'Les chaussures pour le sport'. This merely produced a pair of running spikes and scattered mud over the carpet.

'Mais non, pour le tennis', I pleaded. But this was too much and I found myself outside. The shopkeeper watched me closely until I had gone quite a distance. I saw what I needed in the window of a sports shop around the corner and purchased them at great cost but with no further difficulty.

Once again I wallowed in an expensive hotel bath while the management arranged for my clothes to be cleaned. I slept wonderfully until just after dawn when after a bite to eat I set off in my com-

fortable tennis shoes which gave me a bouncing gait. The motto of
the great family of Josselin is: 'King I cannot be. Prince I would not
deign to be. I am Rohun.' On passing his door I thought that the
proud shopkeeper must be a member of the family but on the distaff
side. I thought of writing a note to this effect on a brick and throwing
it through his bedroom window but desisted because of the *Entente
Cordiale*.

The hawthorn bushes that lined the road were full of goldfinches
in their harlequin dress, flicking buds from one to the other like an
inexpert handball team. The sun shone from a clear sky and I was
sure that it wouldn't rain, the main hazard with my new footwear. By
mid-morning I had reached a famous landmark in Anglo-French
poor relations, *la Colonne des Trentes*. At least the column is famous
in France. The English do not seem to have heard of it.

In 1351 Edward III's knights were swashbuckling about France
cockahoop after their victory at the battle of Crécy. With the rest of
France under English domination the knights could not understand
that Brittany had not been part of the victory, that the province was
ruled by Duke Jean the Good and not by the vanquished King Phil-
ippe VI of Frnce.

'Exasperated by English pillaging and insolence', commences my
guide book, 'thirty Breton knights met a similar number of English
knights by mutual arrangement to decide by combat who would rule
Brittany, Edward or Jean. The battle raged all day during which ten
English and four Bretons were slain, a count of heads deciding in
favour of Jean the Good, but not before one of the Breton knights
had encouraged his thirsty chief with the inspiring exhortation:
"Drink you blood, Beaumanoir, and your thirst will soon pass".'

The column is the latest in a succession of stones which have
marked the spot of the Breton victory ever since, the French having
adopted the victory as they have the country. Each memorial has
been larger than its predecessor, being thrown down and put up by
rival factions on the time-honoured principle of 'you are too big for
me so I'll kick your horse when you are not looking'. The original
cross was knocked down at the end of the sixteenth century by
Roman Catholics who thought their king was being too kind to Pro-
testants. The replacement was destroyed by Breton extremists who
did not like the king whatever his religious views. Its successor was
stolen by offended Revolutionaries but put up again by a Royalist
faction.

This modest cross still stands but it is entirely dominated by the great memorial to the British defeat erected in 1819 by that ungrateful fat man Louis XVIII for whom the British had twice beaten Napoleon to keep him on the throne. This to my mind demonstrates a basic difference in attitude between the two nations. The British lose sleep about whether the existence of Waterloo Station or Trafalgar Square might offend her powerful partner in the European Economic Community. While at the same time the flinty-hearted old French are purging their language of Englishisms such as '*le* weekend', '*le* parking' and '*le* water closet'.

Although the Colonne des Trentes does bear the names of the combatants it seems intended less to glorify the fallen than the erector's noble house. The most important lettering reads: 'Long live the King. The Bourbons for ever'. To this evocaton a visitor had added 'balls' in chalk which seems to sum up the British point of view rather well. But maybe this comment had nothing to do with dislike of a personality but a distaste for the tea biscuit which readily comes to British mind whenever 'bourbon' is mentioned.

To escape the traffic on the main highway I struck off to the southwest into the country toward the hamlet of Travoléon. A track took me along the northern bank of the Oust and kept well clear of Ploermel. With lungs full of fresh air this largish town had no interest for me other than it is supposed to have been named for Saint Armel who destroyed a dragon there in the sixth century.

This is a Christian morality story about a man who never existed although his tomb is supposed to be around somewhere. 'Armel' is Frenchified Breton for '*Arz Mael*' meaning 'prince bear', possibly a connection with Arthur or the Celtic bear deity.

Armel is such a pretty name that it is very popular in Brittany, but strangely enough it is always given to girls. The combination of a dragon and the feminizing of a brave warrior would be too much excitement for my travelling companions so to keep them happy I kept well clear of the place.

This diplomacy failed for I had scarcely been walking for another two hours when there was a shriek of horror from Gildas and a rattle of arms from Arthur. Blocking our path was the largest dolmen I had so far seen, its great weathered slabs glowing white in the sunlight. Gildas made a hurried sign of the cross at this pagan monstrosity and vanished into the underbrush, while Arthur unslung his great shield and prepared to do battle. The Celts believed that the dolmens were entrances to the 'Otherworld', the haunt of unwanted gods, demons, living dead and other unpleasant creatures. One old Welsh poem takes Arthur and three shiploads of men down into the Otherworld to steal a magic cauldron. Only seven returned.

I couldn't see Arthur making the sign of the cross. And one doubts whether he would have gone to church at all. The monks always made him out to be decently Christian, or at least not positively pagan, but there seeems to be an undercurrent suggesting that although Arthur might have been induced to pop something in the offertory box he would be already planning how to steal it back again with interest when God wasn't looking. More likely Arthur's real religion would have been the pre-Christian Celtic one, and his priest would have been a Druid rather than a monk.

Not very much is known about Druidism, that is what has not been got at with Christian spring cleaning but some idea of what the Druids were about has survived.

These holy men of the Celtic religion needed no churches or temples but worshipped in the open air, in forest clearings, by lakes, rivers, streams and springs. Their gods were essentially of the sky, of water, of the air itself. There doesn't seem to have been a clear line drawn between religion, culture and everyday activities and the Druids held absolute power over the lives of the people. This mixture of temporal and secular authority would be similar to the Archbishop of Canterbury turning up at Wembley to stop the Cup Final because he did not like the colour of the scarves. The Druids were not only priests but judges, lawmakers, philosophers, doctors, bards and even warriors. They could at whim condemn to death or excommunicate which was just as bad because a man deprived of tribal protection was hunted down like an animal.

The Druids committed their lore and ritual to memory during many years of training at one of several regular academies. One of the largest was in France, although it was said that the main religious centre was Britain. The Druids did have writing but they seemed to have preferred feats of memory as this trained the mind for philosophical deliberations. Unkindly it was also said that in this way an outsider could not learn their mumbo-jumbo. There is no real evidence that they wore white robes and ritually cut mistletoe with golden scythes but these ideas must have come from somewhere and it's nice to think that they did.

The Druids believed that the souls of the dead passed into other bodies in a kind of immortality. There was no equivalent of the Christian Hell or roastings for the wicked after death but only a land of perfect happiness variously called 'The Land of Eternal Youth', 'The Isle of the Blest' or something similarly attractive.

But if the classical writers are to be believed the Druids indulged in frightful religious rites which were the terror of the living. Even Caesar, whose own nation was renowned for cruelty and bloodletting, was horrified. At least he said so, making no small issue that the reason for the Roman conquest of other lands was to put an end to the Druids and all their works.

These included a large number of human sacrifices by burning them alive in images to the deities to be placated. There was much to do with blood-stained altars, ordeals by fire or water, and the offering of human heads. The worse annual slaughter was at Samain at the beginning of November, one of the four main festivals, to propitiate the spirits of famine in the hope of survival through the harsh, unfruitful months of winter.

The Otherworld was not all bad and it has been suggested that its reputation as the haunt of horrid spectres was a later Christian implantation to turn prospective converts off the place. The Otherworld was also described as a kind of Celtic Valhalla, where time had no meaning in earthly terms, a year might last a minute or a minute an eternity. These legends make it out to be a land of undiluted pleasure, of perpetual happiness and non-stop music, feasting, fornication and the more violent social activities traditionally dear to the hearts of Celts, unlimited brawling and opportunities to get killed. But death or frightful wounds were no hardship for everyone came back to life or full vigour the following day. This belief in the happy land was so strong that the Celts were entirely fearless in battle. Caesar said that his enemies seemed determined to join the party as soon as possible, that is if a more immediate earthly frolic was not in the offing.

The bardic themes give us an insight into what was expected of the likes of Arthur and his men. The characters of the legends were bands of adventurers unable to fit into the normal life of a tribe. They were mercenaries and hunters, a mobile force ready to take up the sword for any ruler who needed help, or for any beautiful woman for that matter.

These warriors were skilled in swordplay, music, poetry, arts, and magic. They were continually on the move, travelling from combat to combat. They crossed to distant lands, to magical islands, even to the Otherworld, either at the invitation of a god or unofficially to steal his fabulous treasure. Entrance to the Otherworld was normally by secret passages from dolmens and earth mounds, the graves of earlier peoples.

These voyages were pure Celtic heroics for the living had a dread of these lonely graves. By these at certain times of the year terrible spectres left their domain and wandered abroad in the land of the living. This horrible breed included the *ankou*, imps, demons, giants, dwarves and ghosts, all the supernatural beings that the older Bretons believe in today, but say they don't after glancing about them quickly.

The Travoléon dolmen was an example of the legendary link with the Otherworld. It is known locally as 'the dolmen of the hole' and an underground passage is said to run from here to an earthwork some kilometres away. But like most Cornish tunnels which are said to connect sea caves with public houses the secret passage does not exist.

Seeing that it was near midday and to give Gildas and Arthur time to collect themselves I sat down on a rock near the dolmen and took out bread, cold sausage and a bottle of wine from my haversack. Wine always seems to act like an Aladdin's lamp on old Bretons for one appeared through the trees and with a polite greeting sat down beside me. I offered him a drink which he refused but took anyway. He told me about the secret passage.

I said that I had looked carefully but couldn't find the hole. The old man nodded sympathetically and said he had never found it either, only the old folk said it was there and personally he did not believe the story. No Breton actually believes these kind of stories himself. It is always 'the others' and 'the old folk'. My new acquaintance must have been all of eighty years old.

'Maybe it is only there sometimes,' he added with Celtic logic.

'Why do you say that?' I asked him curiously. He grunted but did not reply. I did not press him. Better to remain silent in the hope the information you are seeking will come out. Persistent questioning dries them up. The Breton is naturally talkative but he fears the mocking laughter of outsiders which comes all too readily in modern France. I could see that he was turning the matter over in his mind, whether to tell me at all or composing an explanation that would not invite ridicule.

At length he told me about the women, 'only the women and these

were fools anyway' he told me hastily. The women believed that the
'little people' who lived in the hole would steal a new born baby if an
offering of food was not made. They brought nine apples to the dolmen and left them there. If they were gone in the morning then all
would be well. In the old days they used to boil the apples and chant a
little spell which ran:

'If I live to be a hundred you will never come after this pot has
boiled.'

'Do any of the women still do that?' I asked.

'No, no, of course not,' said the old man. He was uneasy and telling me the story had cost him a lot so as a parting gift I gave him my
old walking shoes. He took them without a word, saying that he had
a lettuce at home if I needed one. An exchange of gifts is automatic in
Brittany. But I had no need of lettuces and refused. Instead he gave
me a packet of cigarette papers.

I continued across country for the rest of my journey, across
plough, rough pasture and gorse, arriving at Trehorenteuc just
before nightfall. The ex-miller was right about the abundance of
Arthur. On my right as I entered the village was a signpost directing
me to 'The Valley of No Return'. But it was rather late and I thought
such a despondent invitation might be best left until the following
morning.

Paimpont is nothing less than eight thousand hectares of Gallic
impudence. The great forest with its silent clearings, lakes, and castles is a vast natural Disneyland proving that King Arthur of the romances was a Frenchman. 'The Valley of No Return' was where
Morgane, King Arthur's sister, after an unhappy love affair, took
her revenge by setting up an open air seraglio for erring errant
knights, baiting her trap with drink and dancing girls who wove a
spell that prevented them from returning to their own loves. At Com-
per Castle is Sir Lancelot's academy, the lake in which the fairy Viviane trained him to be 'the best knight in the world' so that he might
quest the Holy Grail. But he wasted his talents, coming back to the
lake after twenty years of misconduct to be greeted by the scathing
retort from his fairy mentor:

'Go back to your Queen. You are not wanted here.'

Close to an ancient iron foundry in the heart of the forest is 'The
Bridge of Secrets' where Lancelot kept his shady trysts with Queen

Guinevere, Arthur's faithless wife. And at Barenton is 'Merlin's Spring' which according to the romances was very cold but nevertheless boiled. And the castles of 'Beaurepaire' and 'Adventurous', and 'The Field of Tournament' where Sir Yvain and Sir Gawain jousted for three days and three nights. And a horseshoe-shaped tumulus called 'Merlin's Grave'.

All these sites are picturesquely appropriate but the inventions of a school of local writers who, like Tennyson and Scott, took a literary wallow in medieval chivalry during the nineteenth century. The signposts of these enthusiasts were later perpetuated by the official French authority for '*monuments historiques et sites*'.

Even the Church seems to have given its blessing. The stained glass of the small chapel at Trehorenteuc instead of representing the Last Supper depicts King Arthur and his knights at the Round Table at the moment of the apparition of the Holy Grail. This is recent and so are the paintings showing the Stations of the Cross which depict Morgane as the personification of Lust, the work of two German prisoners of war in 1945.

Arthur and Gildas were reluctant to climb the hill to the Valley of No Return for on the summit was a large tumulus said to be sacred to the Druids. I left them at the foot of the track by a medieval gatehouse which in the casual Breton way was being used as a byre for cattle.

The local abbé had marked the route by painting white arrows on the red shale of the hill but most of these had been worn away and I was soon lost. To make matters worse it started to rain which did no good to my canvas shoes for as the flood ran down the hill it picked up particles of red dust dyeing them a brilliant pink. No wonder the Druids were fascinated by the place for the hill appeared to be running with blood. In the end I had to ask a man cutting gorse where I could find the Valley of No Return but he didn't smile as I thought he might. The valley is a steep, wide chasm and completely inaccessible because of prickly underbrush. There is said to be a lake at the bottom but I couldn't get to it and I could hear no girlish laughter from Morgane's Bunny Girls so I didn't bother. After three hours of floundering through prickles I managed to rejoin my two companions at the bottom of the hill.

Merlin's Spring was far more accessible, requiring only an easy stroll through the forest but I got little enjoyment from it. The trees were laid out in formal ranks like a wooden army. Pine forests are seldom satisfactory as nature reserves. The stick-like trunks and branches provide scant nesting or defence against hunting kestrels and apart from the distant drumming of a woodpecker there was an eerie silence. This relentless replanting of conifers at the expense of oak or beech will soon have Northern Europe looking as it did in the Ice Ages.

But I have an antipathy for pine trees, particularly Breton ones, because they made me the laughing stock of an entire fish cannery, not to say a considerable portion of the port of Audierne. I had just returned from a month's voyage to the Azores as a member of the crew of a tunnyboat. I was tired and dirty and wanted to go home but the skipper insisted on taking me with him to the cannery to lend moral support while he debated with the *directeur* how many tunny went into cans and how many went to the market. This is always decided before a voyage but there was the matter of weight and cost and anyway the Bretons love an argument.

The *directeur* was wily and seeing the intention was to outnumber him he closed his office door quickly leaving me outside. So I was hanging about in the large gutting and preparing hangar, full of conveyors and running water and old ladies in lace coifs and younger ones in lipstick who sliced away at the fish with knives and eyed me like wolves would do a lamb. It is likely they knew all about me for Brittany is that kind of place but one old dear seized the opportunity to see if any more skeletons could be uncovered.

The Bretons are masters at questioning. They are not obvious, the piece of information they want to extract never forms a part of the first question. The opening gambit was one about where I actually lived in Lervily. This was just to get me talking. I wearily told her that I owned the cottage next to the field with a large pine in the middle of it. I sensed rather than saw the arrestation of movement along the length of the conveyor. The old lady's solemn eyes widened and her expression grew graver.

'Is that so, monsieur?' she said. I thought I saw the suggestion of a wink at her companions but thought nothing of it at the time. She asked me if living next to a pine did not worry me.

A strange question but I replied there was nothing to it. I was used to pines. We had lots of pines in England, and in Scotland they were even bigger. Scots pines they were called, I added. There was a general murmur of wonder but fortunately before I could warm to the subject my skipper returned and we left. As I slid the hangar door

shut I thought I heard a great roar of laughter but I could not connect it with anything I had said. I was wrong. One of the male porters
told me later that I had provided the ladies with one of the funniest
experiences of their lives. Making the usual mistake I had Frenchified the English word 'pine' in the hope it would do service. It hadn't,
for 'peen' in French means 'penis'.

Merlin's Spring was a disappointment. It was much smaller than I
had imagined, hardly larger than the average bath tub and the clearing had been got at by empty bottle and wastepaper distributors and
the Plastic Beaker Folk. The water was clear and very cold but if it
did appear to boil it was due to air bubbles. There certainly did not
seem much magic about it. Still, some people visit cathedrals and are
bored, while others take up the cloth. And the Barenton spring,
unlike the other invented sites, had been a fascination for centuries.

The spring is reputed to act differently for different people. In
times of drought a few drops of water sprinkled on the nearby rock
known as 'Merlin's Stone' is supposed to bring rain. That is if you
believe and you are pure in heart. If not, the rite, like it had for Yvain,
conjures up thunder, lightning, gales and storms, and hail like
machine gun bullets and as deadly. Until the practice was banned by
papal edict in 1853 the local curé used to lead an annual pilgrimage
to the spring to water the rock and to pray. Local legend says that
Barenton could cure all manner of things, particularly diseases of the
eyes.

The strangest event in the history of Barenton indeed may have
inspired Wace the Norman. His visit and the manifestation of Merlin
to an anchorite who lived beside the spring coincide remarkably in
time. Wace wrote about the wizard in 1146 and only a few years
before the hermit called Éon d'Étoile had taken up residence in the
forest at an ancient ruin reputed to have once been a Druid training
college. This is well documented and not a matter of legend.

The hermit began to experience a series of identical visions in
which the wizard Merlin came to him and told him:

'*Per eum qui venturus est judicare vivos et mortuos*' meaning 'He
who comes judges the living and the dead'. Éon, no doubt with an eye
on fame and profit, taking 'eum' or 'he', as a garbled version of his
own name, had set up in business, selling dispensation to sinners,
and there was a mad rush for Merlin told him that the Day of Judgement was fast approaching.

Soon there was a thriving and prosperous establishment at Barenton, staffed by disreputable monks who lived in such grand style and depravity that the news spread to Pope Eugene III at Rheims who personally put a stop to the rival venture. Éon was thrown into a papal prison to learn the error of his ways and his seminary pulled down. The only building to survive was a small chapel which eventually fell down of its own accord. The site was marked by a cross but this too disappeared sometime before 1840.

The area has one other historical association with the Arthur story. Paimpont are the ruins of a great monastery where Henry II, the great profiteer from the Plantagenet propaganda about Arthur, spent fifteen years of tutelage under the monks. Paimpont is no more than fifteen minutes' gallop from Barenton and it would be incredible if his close association with Wace the poet did not spark off some conversation about the mystical qualities of the area and its connection with Arthurian characters if not with Arthur himself. One of the romances had Arthur visiting the spring with a mighty army where it banqueted for ninety days and nights from a table which magically kept replenishing itself.

Out of curiosity I asked an English tourist what he made of it all. It was rather a pointless question for he appeared to be in an advanced state of hysteria, grinding his teeth and flapping his hands as if the Americans had run off with Buckingham Palace. By way of reply he handed me with trembling hands what he described as 'complete and utter bullshit'. It was a leaflet issued by the Paimpont Syndicat d'Initiative which explained the façade was due to the fact that King Arthur had come to Brittany after 'the battle of Salisbury', whatever that was.

According to the enraged Britisher this was rubbish and piffle for King Arthur had never been to France and it was a gross liberty that a pack of 'frogs' should be allowed to get away with it. This chap knew all about King Arthur for he'd recently seen a programme about him on television. I hadn't seen the programme but if the angry gentleman reported it correctly it must have been a masterpiece of oversight and ignorance. My countryman had never even heard of a Celtic Arthur.

Another completely different explanation was given in a small booklet privately printed by the abbé of Trehorenteuc. He wrote that the King Arthur story was brought to Brittany by Breton knights who fought under William the Conqueror at Hastings. He is a kindly, sweet old man and I have met him several times, but I could not bring myself to tell him that at the time of the famous battle none of the romances had been written.

Looking for a place to eat before catching the bus to Dubglas I was walking towards a likely cafe when I saw a large brown dog outside. From inside I heard something which sounded like '*The Virgins of Camaret*' being played with inaccuracy and enthusiasm on bagpipes and *bombarde*. I fled before it was too late.

4 Dubglas

West France, most of which is Brittany, resembles the profile of a wolf's head. The erect ear is Normandy's Cherbourg peninsula from which northern Brittany runs westward as a flattish crown, the long snout terminating in the Isle of Ushant. Under the snout are the gaping jaws of the Brest estuary, complete with thrust out tongue which is the Camaret peninsula. The lower jaw is Finistère, France's Land's End. Along the wolf's crown flows the English Channel meeting the Atlantic Ocean at the snout. The neck and chest of our hypothetical wolf curves down to Spain as the Bay of Biscay.

The River Glein was at the base of the throat. From there we had travelled north-east through the Landes in the middle of the neck to Paimpont. My bus took me north and west to Dubglas, about 160 kilometres distant. The ex-miller had warned me about the tortuous routes taken by Brittany's bus companies and this one was getting the most out of a comparatively short distance by back-tracking and meandering in general. There seemed to be no town in Brittany that we didn't visit once or twice. The driver, reduced by law to a low speed, wore a ferocious scowl which made the notice warning the passengers not to talk to him superfluous. At Rostronon my frustration and a helpful ticket inspector induced me to change buses. I waited an hour before the connection thundered up in a cloud of exhaust. To my intense surprise the driver was my old friend of the ferocious scowl. I had invited the inspector to shorten my journey. He had done so but not speeded it up. Queer things like this are always happening in Brittany.

So I had plenty of time to contemplate the countryside, slumbering as it was under the dim spring sun as it has done for a million years. Except near the coast and the onslaught of the gales of Biscay Brittany has always been a land of forest, woods and copses with pasture in between. But now we have the chain saw and there is a mechanical gale in the trees and very soon they will be gone.

Around Rostronon the look of the land turns from Herefordshire to Sussex but to our left instead of the chalk is the great granite ridge called the Black Mountains. This is the southern finger of the Montagnes d'Arée which points towards the coast to form the wolf's lower jaw in our analogy. The northern finger points towards Ushant.

The Black Mountains are not high but in a generally low, if not flat, country they are impressive, a dark curtain draped across the southern horizon. I had places to go before Dubglas and as I wanted to approach it on foot I left the scowling driver at Châteauneuf-du-Faou, at the foot of the Black Mountains and in a crook of the beautiful Aulne river.

Most old places have spectres which appear to give warning of approaching trouble. Maybe these spectres are more a manifestation of general unease than any desire by the Otherworld to provide a free early warning system. But Châteauneuf-du-Faou — 'faou' means beech trees in Breton — not only has spectres but a whole army of them.

The locals tell you that before both the Kaiser and Hitler Wars the Black Mountains ran loud with ghostly battle cries and the sounds of thousands of horsemen advancing in series of ranks. So runs the Legend '. . . six by six, three by three, and two by two, following the black banners fluttering in the wind of Death . . .' This vast spectral army is Arthur and his men who come to Brittany's aid when she is in peril.

My informant in the restaurant bar was inclined to be cynical about the efficacy of Arthur's army as the German panzers had overrun Brittany in 1942 without much bother from him. I wanted to put the matter to my Arthur but he made himself scarce. His obvious defence would have been that he could not have been the Arthur concerned as he was a foot soldier and never had cavalry according to the experts. The disgruntled disbeliever in the cafe thought that the noise in the Black Mountains might be due to unemployed quarrymen on the rampage.

He had a point. The châteaux of the Loire or of any part of France for that matter all have a distinguishing feature which you can't quite put your finger on until it is pointed out to you and then you wonder why you hadn't noticed all along. It is the conical slated roofs of the towers and turrets. What made the construction of the faultless cones possible were the tiny mutton-chop shaped slates from the quarries around Châteauneuf. British and German slates, said the old quarryman in the café, are about four times the size so such tight cones are not possible.

I contemplated asking him about King Ludwig's fairy tale castles of Bavaria but Germany is still a touchy subject in France and anyway in general the Bretons are unimpressed, if not angered, by contrary evidence. 'Now the tiles come from anywhere', shouted the old quarryman, 'from Portugal, Spain and Ireland, and these are plastic squares only good for the flat roofs of the cement boxes that people live in today.'

The old man told me that he was the only real slate napper left in the area, the rest had gone off to the United States and Canada. He was joined at the bar by another slate napper who, no doubt, would have eventually claimed that he was the only real slate napper left in the area, so I slipped out into the gathering dusk to see the 'Virgin in the Tree' who wouldn't be bothered by slates whatever the size.

The Druids are supposed to have held the oak tree in deep reverence. The village oaks of England, sometimes elms, the traditional meeting places of the village parliaments are probably a survival of this cult. Just outside Châteauneuf on the road to Laz near the banks of the Aulne is an old oak tree which appears to have been 'Christianized'. Carved into the bole of the tree is a recess which holds a statue of the Virgin Mary. Perhaps this figure should not have been the mother of Jesus Christ at all but his grandmother for elsewhere such combinations are invariably known as 'Anne in the Tree'.

There is no mention in the Bible that Jesus had a grandmother called Anne so the preservation of such a personage in the Christian religion is possibly due to the Christian habit of taking over rather than knocking a pagan deity. Ana or Anu was a Celtic goddess, indeed the most powerful female one as the high place she holds in the Christian pantheon suggests. She was the earth mother, the spirit of earth and water, and almost everything else. The hills in County Kerry in Ireland are known as the 'paps' or 'breasts of Anu'.

The *lavoirs* of France are watched over by a Virgin in a recess and this has given rise to the speculation that Mary was a later and possibly mistaken replacement for Saint Anne who herself usurped Anu. Another adoption into the Christian religion is Saint Brigit or Bride who is thought to be a duplication of Anu. Such duplications, even triplications, were common in the old religion of the Celts. Danu,

Anu, and Brigit are thought to be the same goddess, all sharing the same role as the deity of plenty and fertility. Brigit, however, always had a literary bent, being also the deity of culture and learning.

Before dinner and bed I had intended to see the sixteenth century stained glass window at the small chapel of Notre Dame du Crann said to have been inspired by Albrecht Dürer. Rumour has it that the glass was actually executed by the great German artist himself but this seems unlikely as such valuable art treasures are not likely to be wasted on rural Brittany. The chapel door was locked, for like elsewhere old church ornaments are being relentlessly pillaged, but a hand-written notice on the door did recommend knocking if I wanted to look round.

At last the door was opened slightly by an old and snappy nun who demanded to know what in the name of the devil I wanted, an inappropriately phrased question I thought under the circumstances. I pointed to the notice which the '*bonne soeur*' smartly tweaked from its drawing pin and then withdrew, slamming the door with a bang. So the art world will have to go without my opinion on whether the stained glass is actually by Dürer or not.

From Châteauneuf my somewhat circuitous route to Dubglas curved first north then west like a reversed question mark. I was feeling very stiff from welking but the canvas shoes, atthough still bright pink from the slate at Paimpont and sparking off a great deal of comment from passers-by, were ideal and the blisters were healing. And the larks were barking at heaven high in the cloudless blue sky and I felt as buoyant as they.

Some fourteen kilometres on I passed through the largish village of Lannedern — the 'parish of Saint Edern.' As may have been gathered Brittany has always been very generous with the title and has thousands of saints unknown to the rest of Christendom and sniffed at by Rome. But 'saint' originally only meant 'holy' and most of them could be said to have been that whether they were monks or Druids.

Edern does, however, have the distinction of being known outside Brittany. There is a Bodedern in Anglesey, in North Wales. He even appears as one of Arthur's peculiar companions in *Culhwch and Olwen* and his credentials as a Christian seem very dubious for he is the son of Nudh — the Celtic god Nodens under another name. Another of Nudh's sons is Gwynn who was master of Hell and the nasty spirits which sneak out of the dolmens at midnight. It could be a coincidence but a few kilometres from Lannedern is Botmeur

Marsh which the local Bretons know as 'The Gates of Hell'. But you can't get the locals to talk objectively about Botmeur for it is also the site of a vast nuclear power station which they rightly or wrongly, have been led to believe by hostile pamphleteers means cancer, leukaemia, and slow poisoning of their food.

If the Bretons can extract any humour out of what they vociferously consider to be a potentially murderous liability on their doorstep it is the innocence displayed by the planners in their choice of the marsh for the reactor despite its traditionally evil reputation. The locals almost seem eager for a disaster so they will be proved right.

A splendid example of how French cartographers change Breton place names because of their different shaped eardrums was the next small village on my route. On the map it is Guimiliau. In fact this should be Gwikmeliaw, pronounced 'Gooeekrachmeliaoo' so you can't blame the Frenchmen really.

Meliaw was a sixth-century prince of Brittany's Cornwall known for his generosity and wisdom. But his wicked brother Riwod coveted the throne and arranged for him one of those accidental deaths for which the old Celts were famous. Still barring his succession however, was a seven-year-old son, Melar, who should have been quite easy to polish off but Riwod must have considered that two members of the same family torn to pieces by mad hunting dogs might be thought too much of a coincidence. Instead he cut off his nephew's left foot and right hand thus preventing him from mounting a horse and wielding a sword so he lost the throne by default.

But a miracle intervened and the lad grew a silver hand and a bronze foot which continued to grow at the same rate as he did. Perhaps a non-Celt would be unable to guess the end of this story. Riwod's son invited Melar to a feast and hacked off his head while he was in his cups. So there was no happy ending.

There are a considerable number of Celtic legends about men with silver hands and Ludd Llawereint in the *Mabinogion* was spoken of as being 'of the silver hand'. King Nuada of Ireland, similarly incapacitated, was given one by a miracle performed by two 'saints', one a blacksmith, the other a doctor. When Irish monks recorded a legend they were careful to change controversial characters into 'saints'. The names of the two saintly artisans in the Nuada legend, Diancecht and Credne, sound very much like those of Druids.

Christian miracles have to be permanent in order to conform to the ethic of triumph of good over evil, but Celtic miracles were often very temporary affairs. The Celts did not mind a story ending in tragedy for their humour has a melancholy twist. Being as accustomed to hardship and sadness terminal tragedy was for them more like reality. The sad end of Miliaw proves its authenticity and that it has kept it is a tribute to the long folk memories of the Bretons.

The inhabitants of Guimiliau consider their town to be a city, a fact which manifested itself in the high price I was charged for a bed that night. Before being named for Miliaw (this is taking us back quite a bit) reputation has it as 'Kerfeunteun' — 'the town of the spring'. But it was destroyed by Saxons who must have also taken the masonry for there are no remains of its illustrious past still visible.

The expense of the night's lodging was offset by an unexpected windfall that I received that afternoon while eating my bread and cheese at the passage grave near Commana, really '*cwm—Ana*', another reminder of the earth mother. These megalithic graves are formed of slabs of stone and as the name suggests resemble rectangular tunnels. They are invariably known in Brittany as 'houses of the little people' — *Ty a Korrigans*. This one was no exception and it was labelled as such on a board nailed to a tree. This was examined with great interest by a car load of Parisians who approached me for further explanation. As I say, as I learned most of my French in Brittany I speak it with a Breton accent (the villagers say it is more like a Chinese one) and I am nearly always taken for a local by tourists from metropolitan France. The following dialogue took place:

Weasel-like Papa: 'Pardon, *monsieur*, but what is a Ty ar Korrigan?'

Me: 'The house of a little man about this high — a dwarf in fact.' The weasel jumps backward about a metre in alarm, regards me with astonishment then shoots a 'we've got a wildie here' look at *madame*. He tries again.

Papa: 'But it is a prehistoric grave is it not, *monsieur?*'

Me: 'Of course, but what I mean to say is the chisel marks on the underside of the roof are said to be the clog marks of the little people when they danced. Have a look for yourself.'

The weasel said he wouldn't bother and took a franc piece out of his pocket and handed it to me with a look of sorrow. Then he herded *madame* and the little ones back into the car at great haste. And they drove off with the smell of rubber. I was not at all put out, even thinking that I had stumbled across a supplementary source of income.

But nobody else came to the passage grave before I finished eating. One franc is pretty poor pay for a village idiot. Our one at Lervily earns ten times that in as many minutes. I did not look back but I imagined Arthur and Gildas following me with smug expressions on their faces.

Three hours' brisk walk the following morning took me to Le Martyre. The martyr in question was said to be King Saloman of Brittany who was murdered during a revolt in A.D. 421. This town also has a story of lost glory, but a probably genuine one. From the fourteenth to the eighteenth century it was the most important market for horses, cattle and textiles in the whole of western France, with merchants coming from England, Ireland and Belgium. But after the Revolution they went elsewhere.

There is an interesting inscription on the wall of the church ossuary — a storehouse for the bones of the long dead. It says in Breton:

'The death, the judgement, the cold Hell, when man thinks of these things he should tremble.'

This notion of a *cold* as opposed to a flaming Hell is not unusual in Brittany. One wonders whether this is due to the Celtic concept of that part of the Otherworld called Anaon — a freezing purgatory. But it might just be due to the effect on rural people of the bitter gales of winter. Starving, huddled round a small fire, vicariously a hot Hell might even be an attractive proposition and not much of a deterrent.

From Le Martyre to Landerneau is but an hour and a half's steady saunter. It lies at the head of the lovely valley of the River Elorn but despite this the citizens have a reputation for rapacity and are usually described by the almost universal label for money grabbers and cheats as 'horse dealers'.

Landerneau is the ancient capital of the old principality of Leon but in fact only half the town is actually in Leon, the other is in Cornwall. The Leonais traditionally are dupers and the Cornish the duped and there are countless stories told by one about the other. The Leonais say the head of the town lies in Leon and the arse in Cornwall. The Cornish rejoinder to this is the pointed question: 'Just passing through?'.

The old name is Lanternoc, believed to be named for Saint Enoch. He was one of the numerous saints whom Breton hagiographers have crossing Brittany in a stone trough. These stone trough voyages of the saints, being in ridiculous defiance of Archimedian principles, are always taken as something of a joke caused by monkish taste for the miraculous. But maybe the truth lies in a misunderstanding of the nature of the craft in which the holy men arrived in Brittany.

The craft of the sixth century must have been currachs, wicker framed, hide-covered vessels, still used by some Irish coastal fishermen and in the Welsh marshes in the form of corracles. Stability for long sea voyages was achieved by stone ballast and if these frail craft were wrecked, as they invariably would have been on arriving on the rocky Breton shores, the ballast would be all that remained. Old legends do refer to these vessels as 'boats of stone' and from this stone trough would be a short mental leap for the monk chroniclers.

At the old church of Landerneau is a kind of monument to artistic licence and Christian frugality. The story goes that a poor sculptor was commissioned to carve in stone the evils that might beset the parishioners in their daily commerce. No price for the work was agreed but payment would be on results. The monks rubbed their hands with pleasure at the prospect for the sculptor's clothes were ragged and he was hungry. Any objection would see the artist on his way with nothing but a kick up the backside for his pains.

To exemplify 'Greed' the sculptor carved a pig, to which interpretation the monks raised an immediate objection on the grounds that the pig was a dirty and disgusting animal and unfit to adorn a holy building. For the work the poor man received nothing. The portrayal of 'Theft' — a man running away with a sack of corn — was greeted with even more animosity, possibly justifiable in this case for the thief bore a resemblance to the abbot. For this day's work the poor man received nothing. The sculptor left immediately after he had finished the third carving without saying a word and was never seen again. The final figure in the tableau representing 'Cunning' showed a fox preaching to some young chicks. There was no doubt about the artist's intention for the fox was dressed in a habit and cowl. The angry monks chiselled away the fox but inexplicably left the chicks and the label 'Cunning' with the result that ever since visitors to the church must regard their poultry with suspicion.

Just outside the town on the northern bank of the Elorn is a ruined câstle which by rights should have been at Paimpont for it is known as the Château de Joyeuse-Garde. It is said to have been the fortress of Tristram and temporary refuge of Sir Lancelot to which King Arthur laid siege in order to get Queen Guinevere bank. According to the romance Lancelot must have lived on love alone for the siege was protracted until the personal intervention of an envoy at Rome.

You find yourself wondering how the ruin became associated with the Arthurian cycle for the river of the romance was called the 'Ombre' which in English translations is taken to mean 'the river of shadows'. But '*ombre*' is also the name of the fish we call the grayling and there are any amount of grayling in the river.

More interesting is the connection in local memory with Tristram. Tristram, it may be remembered, was a character of Breton legend who was adopted into the later Arthurian romances. He is always called Tristram of Lyonesse, Lyon or Lyens, always taken to be a mythical land placed somewhere off the coast of Britain's Cornwall. If there ever was such a place it sank beneath the waves after the time of the Celtic Arthur.

This is typical of the insular attitude of the British towards the Celtic Arthur. Landerneau is the old capital of Leon and this north-west corner of Brittany is still called Leon. So Tristram's birthplace is neither legendary nor sunken, though it could be said to be off the coast of Cornwall.

Contrary evidence that Tristram was a Breton is the existence of a two metre high stone at Menabilly in England's Cornwall. A vertical Latin inscription tells us that:

Tristram (Drusanus) lies here, the son of Conomor (Conomori).

In fact he doesn't as the fallen stone was found a hundred metres or so further north and was later erected at the new site. But if Tristram was buried anywhere in the vicinity how can I argue that he was a Breton? This one is easy. Legend has Tristram in exile waiting for the boat with the white sail which he hoped would bring his beloved Iseult and people do not get exiled to their homeland. The boat was coming from Brittany.

British authorities admit that they can't identify Conomor, Tristram's father in the inscription on the stone. But the Breton legends are full of him. For the writers of saints' lives he is the archetypal blackguard, a hatpeg on which to hang all kinds of mischief, skulduggery, wickedness, and blasphemy. We will meet Conomor later.

It was on the road south to Pen Bran that a stupid slip of my tongue offended a kindly priest who stopped his car to ask me if I wanted a lift. I'm sure what attracted him was my pink footwear. It looked as if blood had seeped through the canvas and caked on the outside. Maybe the priest thought I was doing some kind of penance. After looking down at my feet he asked me if by chance I were Catholic and without thinking I replied I wasn't, that in fact I was a Christian. Maybe I was preoccupied with Chrétien de Troyes. This did not please the priest and he climbed back into his car muttering that Catholics were good Christians too and that I'd be one too if it wasn't for Henry VIII.

Pen Bran, or 'Bran's Head' has a mystical association in Celtic legend. One of the *triads* has Arthur wickedly digging up the head of Bran, a talisman against invasion. The god Bran appears in the legends of both Wales and Ireland. He is always referred to as Bran the Blessed. He seems to have been a giant with enormous stature and strength. His nose was said to be as large as a mountain and his eyes were like twin lakes.

Bran was engaged in a mighty war against King Matholwych of Ireland. In fact he laid his body across the Irish Sea so that his army could cross over. But in his final battle with the king, Bran is wounded in the foot by a poisoned arrow and realizing that he is dying the doughty warrior has his head struck off and taken to London and buried facing the Continent so that it would ward off any invaders.

By some strange quirk 'bran' has come to mean a crow or a raven. In Celtic times the ritual burial of the bird's head was also considered to keep attackers away. It would be surprising if the ravens at the Tower of London had nothing to do with this belief. And the existence of the tiny hamlet of Pen Bran, I like to believe, has something to do with the great bay I could now see as I crested the hill on which the hamlet stands. Arthur's next four battles, themselves successful defences against Saxon invasion, were fought near here.

Since the Nennius manuscript came to light, although controversy has raged over where the River Dubglas actually was, some kind of agreement seems to have been reached that the name comes from the old British word 'dubboglasso' which meant 'blue-black'. This is quite alright for describing something unchangeable like ink but for a river which changes colour like a chameleon it would be useless. One of the fascinating things about water is that it is so changeable. Sediment, the colour of the sky, even wind direction all play their part. (I remember an idiotic argument that Homer must have been blind or at least colour blind because he had written of 'the wine dark sea'. This is a landsman's argument. I have seen the sea as red as blood at times.)

Daoulas in Brittany does not come from 'blue-black' but from an older Celtic word meaning either 'two valleys' or 'two lands'. The latter is the more likely. Dubglas and Daoulas sound exactly the same.

The description 'two lands' is appropriate for here the River Daoulas forms the frontier between the two ancient Breton Kingdoms of Cornwall and Leon. Leon is significant for Nennius says that the Dubglas 'was in the region Linnius' and this must be a Latinization of Leon, Tristram's Lyonesse, Lyon, or Lyens. Nothing sounding like Linnius occurs in Britain, a fact which has generated more scholastic heat than light.

Coming down the Daoulas valley you become aware of the brightening of the sky which marks any great stretch of water, for ahead lies the great Brest estuary, the wolf's jaws of my analogy. This turbulent stretch of water was a kind of home for me. This is where I learned the rudiments of Breton seamanship which I hoped would get me aboard a Breton tunnyman.

There is something uncanny about the stretch of sea from the Isle de Sein up to Ushant. The Bretons call it 'ar mor iraz'. This means 'the angry sea'. All seas become angry but 'ar mor iraz' sneaks it up on you. On a day of flat calm when there is hardly a breath of wind, without any kind of warning, the sea loses its temper. Within an hour the millpond has become a murderous battlefield of cross seas and God help any small craft in the way.

There have been attempts to explain this strange irascibility, possibly some trick of the ebb or flood tide pouring between the skerries and small islands, or maybe the fetch from a storm far out in the Atlantic. Nobody knows for sure. The effect is deadly and it has produced a race of seamen renowned for expertise and temperaments which like their element turn from contemplative melancholy to violence and foul language for no apparent reason other than sheer whim.

When I first sailed to Brittany 'ar mor iraz' tried to drown me, not by the tumult of waves, but an even stranger phenomenon. Sudden fog banks are bad enough but when coupled with lighthouses that cease to shine and fog sirens which can't be heard one begins to suspect witchcraft. To be lost among the countless snaggle-toothed rocks of that terrible coast under these conditions makes you yearn for a tree to sit under. The official pilot book for the area warns of this peculiarity so it's not imagination.

The fishermen have a little prayer which covers the situation:

'*Va doue sikhourit de dramen iraz,*
Rak va lestr a zo bihan hag ar mor a zo braz'.
('Our God protect us through the angry sea
For our boat is so small and the seas are so big.')

Breton fishermen are almost pagan so when they resort to prayer to the Christian god it can be safely said that they are badly frightened.

The river apart there are no less than three places which bear the name Daoùlas — Plougastel, Lagonna and Daoulas by itself. The largest town is Plougastel-Daoulas — 'the ptace of the castle'. Eccording to local legend it was once the largest and finest city in the whole world until it threw out a woman who had given birth to seven children — a number with uncanny associations according to Celtic lore. The sorceress, for she turned out to be one after all, cursed the town. Henceforth Brest would prosper while Plougastel would go into a decline. For every house built, three would fall down. History gives the more prosaic explanation that the town was emptied by the Black Death which swept Europe in the Middle Ages and that it never recovered. The origin of the legend could be the stone baptismal font at the church which is decorated with seven heads. Or maybe the font was based on the legend, I don't know.

t is true however that Brest has flourished instead of Plougastel, but Brest is a good port and Plougastel a bad one, a fact for which the townsfolk should be thankful. Together with most of the inhabitants Brest was destroyed by the bombs and shells of both sides during the Hitler War.

The Bretons have a keen nose for insanity in other people, usually the inhabitants of the next village down the road, whether it be for scratching the head with the left hand or a dislike for the taste of limpets. Plougastel is renowned throughout the region for crabs in the head. They are said to distrust each other intensely. There are families whose only vocal communication for centuries has been a raspberry. The only time they get together is to celebrate All Soul's Day, once again the Samain of Druidism. I have seen the Plougastel ritual and it is more frightening than mad.

The ritual of 'the apple trees' and 'the bread of dead souts' takes place between stretches of water such as between two rivers, with deputations from the clans or families of the neighbourhood. All Soul's

Day is when the families remember their dead loved ones so there is very little of the merriment which normally accompanies Breton gatherings, but even so the ritual is creepy.

Silently the young girls circle in groups distributing apples and medlars, the old people give presents of bread especially baked for the occasion. The Christian view is that the ritual is a communion between the living and the dead, indeed until recently the participants dressed in black and white to represent death or life. Maybe, but to my mind the girls and old men are in fact innocently playing the parts of human sacrifices, the rite is a survival of far more terrible happenings than the giving away of presents of fruit and bread.

I think that Arthur's battles would have been fought a few kilometres to the south west of Daoulas unadorned, as Nennius said, on the banks of the river. The attraction for the Saxons would have been the two great Celtic monasteries, one that stood at Daoulas and the other at Landevennec across the Faou river. The first was said to have been founded by Gildas and both were visited frequently by old red face. Daoulas is no more, in fact both monasteries were destroyed by the Saxons, but Landevennec was rebuilt.

The second Landevennec was built by a local magnate named Wiomarc'h and people bored with stories of the infallibility of the great will love this man for he gave out what was possibly the worst advice in history. No mean distinction. William of Normandy had just landed at Pevensey and it was to Wiomarc'h that he turned for counsel. Wiomarc'h had been a member of Edward the Confessor's court and he knew the Saxons well. And William knew that the terrible Saxons were marching south to meet him, victorious after the battles of Fulford and Stamford Bridge against two powerful foreign invaders. To William's dismay the Breton told him to keep well within his temporary fortifications, for the Saxon army was great and his army would be easily outnumbered and slaughtered to the last man. Better still get back to Normandy while the going was good. As we know, William did not take the advice and pressed inland to fight the Battle of Hastings. Without Hastings we would be still speaking the language of Scandinavia; worse, we would not have the only date most of us can remember.

It is possibly that Wiomarc'h managed to get at the Breton mercenaries with his gloomy forecast. It was the Bretons who broke against the Saxon shield wall and came streaming back down the hill followed by the triumphant defenders who thought they had won. This gave the astute Norman the idea of staging a series of mock retreats for this drew the enemy out from behind their insuperable shield wall and into the open. This tactic helped to win the battle.

From Daoulas down to Penmarc'h is one of the most spectacularly beautiful coasts in the world, rugged and wild with great headlands like granite cathedrals. I had reckoned to walk most of the way for this was my part of Brittany. I was familiar with the land but I had only seen most of it from the sea where picturesque grandeur means danger and anyway you get little time for idling on a fishing boat. I wanted to see it all again, perhaps for the last time, for the cottage in the tiny hamlet of Lervily was no longer mine.

My first mistake was that the coast road is well inland and unless you keep turning off down one of the small tracks the coast is out of sight. There are no paths through the gorse close to the headlands. The second was that I knew the country so well that I got lost.

I cut across the neck of the Camaret peninsula for I had to keep my walking down to some kind of proportion and so I did not experience the virgins of the city and anyway according to 'Ar Mor Braz' they are so few as to be able to hold their annual reunion in a telephone box and still leave room for an orchestra. So I arrived still full of vigour at Plonévez-Porzay.

The patron saint of Plonévez is Saint Anne and there can be no doubt about her pagan origins as earth mother for, here, to her name has been added the title, 'de Palud', which is abbreviated Latin for 'marsh'. An old legend says that she was actually a Breton by birth, and was the widow of a local chief. She was always referred to as 'Hent Anne' or 'Old Anne' or more formally as 'Mamm goz ar Bretoned' — the 'Old Mother of Brittany'.

One version of the legend has the widow departing Brittany for Jerusalem where she meets and marries Joachim, father of Joseph the Carpenter. Once again widowed she returns to the old country to die. No less than Jesus and Saint Peter come to Brittany to pay their last respects.

One suspects that these kinds of story were tales made up for children by a kindly priest which somehow got taken seriously. But we should be careful that in dismissing them as such we are not overlooking something, though for the life of me I can't think what this could be. When first discovered the *Mabinogion* was thought to be just bedtime stories until someone realized their significance.

I was just thinking that I was going along rather well when I realized that instead of Douarnenez I was on the road to Locronan. And I did not like Locronan. There does not seem to be one building in the town where you can't get sold something. Souvenirs, fake Breton statues, curios, pots, pictures, trinkets, and those plastic imitation wood plaques with expensive slogans such as 'Our real friends arrive early and leave late', a thought which must give the average French-man nightmares. But they buy them just the same. Maybe these Tro-jan Horses are bought to give to friends so they have to foot the bill. And when you think you are safe some artist is surreptitiously sketch-ing you or cutting your silhouette out of black paper and getting annoyed when you say you don't want to buy it. It shouldn't really matter for they make you look like the current screen idol and they can always sell it to someone else.

This tourist make-believe is as incomprehensible as fish language. Take the sale of picture postcards which don't look like the place or the people. Even the Bretons are vulnerable to the projection of a fancy dress Brittany. At Tante'phine's I caught one of the villagers buying a postcard which depicted a fake kind of Breton costume. Poking my nose in I told her she should be ashamed of herself. She didn't dress like that. Our local costume is interesting enough and it is genuine and you can see it anytime at Lervily.

She agreed and instead she chose a card showing the fishermen on the quay and I went off thinking I'd struck a blow for reality. Later Tante'phine told me that the old lady had been back and bought her first choice saying that the *Yann-Soaz* should mind his own business. She didn't want to upset the Parisians to whom she was sending the card. They would only know the Bretons as they were expected to look and the fake costume was far prettier.

The town is named for an Irish immigrant named Saint Ronan who came to Brittany in the sixth century. He established his hermi-tage in the forest and performed a large number of miracles. So pow-erful was his magic that barren women gave birth nine months after visiting Ronan's cell. His big rival was a Druidess named Kleben, a dirty word in Breton, but Ronan changed into a wolf and ate her. King Gradlon heard of the feast and was upset because he believed in the old religion and he cast Ronan into prison. But Ronan eased his Queen's problem and on the birth of her child the entire tribe became Christians.

I escaped from Locronan in a large refrigerated fish lorry which had become jammed between two gift shops. I helped to extricate it

and used the opportunity to scrounge a lift to Douarnenez where I'd
wanted to go in the first place. The driver popped into a boutique to
use the telephone and emerged with a silhouette that made him look
like Rudolph Valentino. Angrily he rubbed it hard against his backside and threw it into the gutter.

'Ten francs for that I paid,' he snapped. 'Some fools will buy anything,' he added philosophically.

5 Dulce Domum

Douarnenez is the best fishing port in Southern Brittany, with a reasonably easy approach and deep water in all states of the tide. Deep water is a rare commodity on our coast, otherwise you are continually bolting 'legs' to the hull to save your vessel falling over at low tide. Consequently we shallow water harbour men call the Douarnenists 'woodpeckers' — a term which originated with the green hulls of the port but with overtones that they have less work to do and spend their time yammering.

The Douarnenists call we Audierne men the 'Gwaienenou' which is nothing to do with Sir Gwain of the Round Table but comes from the name of our river, with the implication that our fishermen are safer up it and should not venture far from land. In the old days the Douarnenists had a fearful reputation as brawlers and knife fighters, and so did the Gwaienou — a fact hard to believe now as you can tweak off the caps of fishermen from both ports and jump on them with impunity.

Being a Gwaienenou but at one time working on a 'woodpecker' trawler I mentioned that from what I had heard I was lucky not to be stabbed. This brought vociferous denials from around the bistro table. And I believed them for I was only fooling and my crew were the most peaceful of men. Turning my back to find somewhere to hang my coat and cursing the lack of pegs I was startled when a knife thudded into the woodwork inches from my head.

'Hang it on that,' said the thrower amid guffaws of laughter. So it seems the skill is still there but the malice has gone. The humour was short lived, however, for the thrower got a sound box on the ear from the *madame*, not only for the dangerous nature of the joke but for the damage to the door and the fact that the knife came from the kitchen and the blade might have been bent.

The knife would have had to come from the kitchen for you never see Breton fishermen with anything but folding pocket knives, nothing like the great things resembling small swords I have seen affected by some British fishermen but these are usually young men who'd rather look the part than do the job. The Breton usually has three pocket knives, one for eating with, one for ropework and a smaller version for fish gutting. The last two he is continually sharpening and they are like razors. If there is a requirement for a larger knife, such as for gutting and cleaning tougher fish like the tunny, these are kept in racks aboard the ship and never brought ashore for the gendarmes react quickly to the sight of potentially offensive weapons. But the Bretons are amazingly quick with their pocket knives. Petit Jean from my village could whip out his knife, flick open the blade, cut a rope, close it and return it to his pocket in one sweeping movement in far less time than this sentence took to write.

No doubt the main factor in the pacification of the Breton fishing communities is the law which prevents a skipper from embarking a hand who has been in any kind of trouble with the police, and this includes quite minor sentences for drunkenness or even for arguing with a gendarme. You have to be on your best behaviour for a certificate to this effect has to be produced before you are allowed aboard. And one such misdemeanour will disqualify you for up to three years, a harsh penalty on a coast where there is little alternative employment, and the French are not known for generosity to the unemployed.

But before this law, in the days of low fish prices, near starvation and disillusion, where a piece of leather tacked to clogs had to serve for seaboots, and when bare feet were common, the Breton seamen were a murderous lot. You don't have to be much over forty years old to remember these times. Further back even Nelson's seamen were horrified by the rapacity and venom of the crews of the swift sailing *chasse-marées* which shot out of ports such as Brest and Saint Malo to pluck out an East Indiaman from a convoy and be gone before anything could be done to stop them. When no such prizes were in the offing the Bretons kept their hands in with the sack and burning of ports of the south and south west of England. A fog bank was virtually a warning that the Bretons could be expected.

But today it is hard to imagine these big, good humoured gentle men ever having been involved in such dirty work. Today the piracy is confined to stealing fish and crabs out of Britain's territorial waters, particularly in foggy or bad weather. At least that's what the

Cornish fishermen say, and they must be right.

So when I arrived at Douarnenez with the fish lorry I went to Chez Josée's to see if any of my old knife-fighting friends were about. I missed the cheerful *camaraderie* that I had shared during the winter voyage to the northern seas. It must have been wry humour on the part of the owners whom I had approached with a view to working aboard a tunnyman which fished in the sub-tropics, to send me instead on a cooling off trip to the Arctic Circle. But with *Men Brial*, named for a rock off the Breton coast and built rather like one, I had learned a lot.

Unfortunately the trawler was at sea and so were her sisters and the bistro was empty. But Josée remembered me. And oddly enough someone had been enquiring about me that very morning, a little man who occasionally lived thereabouts, she said, who was looking for a tall Yann-Soaz with a red beard who was walking around Brittany looking for King Arthur. She had told the little man that although she knew of such a Yann-Saoz with a red beard who had worked on a tunnyman she had not connected me with the Arthur seeker until I had walked into the bistro.

Josée may have been surprised at the speed in which I finished my drink and bid her good-bye. But Henri overtook me on the road to Treboul, near the small landlocked island called 'Tristram' after a sixth-century hermit who lived there and maybe nothing to do with the Arthurian character. But it is this river island that gives Douarnenez, meaning 'the land with the island', its strange name.

The little man took up his unique tentative pacing beside me without a word. Instead he shook my hand and handed me a potato. I examined this unusual gift carefully but seeing nothing obviously rare or valuable about it was about to chuck it into the hedge when Henri stopped me with a cry of alarm. If cut in half, he said, the potato would produce five or six kilos easily. I explained that I had no land in which to plant the thing but Henri gave one of those great Breton shrugs of the shoulders with the neck thrusting forward like a tortoise to tell me that my landless state was not his responsibility nor did it detract from the wonder potato's potential. I put it in my pocket to save further debate.

After looking about me I asked him what had happened to my old enemy. Sold, he explained, and at a handsome profit. He jingled some coins in his pocket significantly. Had I known that it was in fact an English shooting dog, a sort which would retrieve, point, and perform all kinds of similar services if, like the potato, I had been astute enough to recognize its potential? He implied that the brute could load a gun and pluck a pheasant if given half a chance.

Actually, continued Henri, warming to the subject in the way Bretons do with a suitable audience, the dog was of the kind that was used by horsemen who hunted with falcons. He had seen one exactly like it on television. Having been defeated in the potato debate I could see no point in telling Henri that the kind of dog he had in mind died out in the eighteenth century, and what he had seen was probably a historical horse opera about Robin Hood.

For all their proximity to their supposed mother country the older Bretons hold some queer ideas about Britain. They seem to have an intellect that has stood still in time somewhere about the Middle Ages. It seems hard to credit but old Jean Jauoin had clogged out of Tante'phine's in a huff because I had argued that tournaments with knights on horseback were no longer the fashion in England. And Jauoin had actually been to London where he had been stationed with a French naval unit during the Kaiser War. I can't explain the reason for this peculiar time slip however much I think about it.

Getting back to Henri, I thought it unfair that as I was supposed to have been the owner of the English hunting paragon that the sale had been made without my permisssion and so far there had been no mention of my share of the profit. But I did not want to appear parsimonious after the gift potato. Maybe that was my share after Henri had deducted his commission.

The wooded road was leading us towards the Point du Raz, the most westerly point in continental Europe, and my wolf's lower jaw. This narrow strip of land is full of dolmens and 'houses of the little people' and tall menhirs. This is pure Druid country and all the saints who have left nothing but their names to the hamlets hereabouts fought dragons and arrived in stone troughs. Despite the large number of pagan monuments there has been very little 'Christianizing'. Perhaps the task was too great but more likely it was thought that such things were best left alone in an area where tradition holds closer to the old beliefs than it does to the religion of Rome.

Such is the spirit of the land that another character joined my little party of mental travellers. I needed a Druid and a bard and it was Taliesin who came to mind. This man is a complete enigma. Literary historians hold that he was one of the bards who might have composed the *Gododdin*, that he was sixth-century and lived in Cumberland.

He hints at such in one of his poems. But the Welsh hold correctly that he appears as a character in *Culhwch and Olwen* of the 'Welsh' Mabinogion. But again it might be argued that as this tale originated in Brittany then he must be Breton.

Nothing or much of Taliesin has survived according to various viewpoints. Take this extract for example:

> I existed as a multitude of things.
> Before I was given substance,
> I was a shadowy sword held in the right hand,
> I believe in that which can be seen,
> But I was a tear drop in the air,
> I was the most brilliant of all the galaxy of stars.
> I was a word in a thousand words.
> I was the original book.
> I was a beam of light...

And the even more wonderful:

> Primary chief bard
> I am to Elphin
> And my original land
> Is the region of the summer stars
> Johannes the diviner
> Called me Myrrdhin...

These extracts from lengthy poems give us something of the essence of the man. It is thought that they are puzzles in which Taliesin is hinting at his identity but in a cussed Celtic way making it too difficult. One intriguing point is that 'Myrrdhin' is the original Breton name for Merlin the Sorceror. The French romancers hurriedly changed this, for '*merde*' means 'shit' in French and is hardly the sort of thing you want in elegant romances about damsels in distress and courtly love.

Not a few authorities say however that Taliesin was no master of allusion, nor mixer of profundity and mischief, but his poems are gibberish and that he was not trying to tell us anything at all. Then of course there is the dumbfounding argument that there was no such person as Taliesin, that the works are those of another bard called Llywarch Hen. Another school of detractors says that the poems are not of the sixth but of the twelfth century. Another that he was merely satirizing the supposed sagacity of the old bards.

If so then he was an expert. Legend has him arriving at the court of
the King of Gwynedd, some say in Wales, others in Brittany, for
there are two. He begins his career more like Flashman than Tom
Brown, taunting the elder bards for doing little but flattering King
Maelgwn. He cast a spell on them so all they could say was 'bleroom
. . . bleroom' which did not please the king mightily.

That's what I liked about my new travelling companion. He is tan-
gible but elusive like mercury. When you think you have him fast in
your hand he has slipped away. Like Brittany he has a will-o'-the-
wispishness, combining levity with sadness, warmth and friendship
with unplumbable and tenuous depths of Breton natures.

Taliesin means 'of the fair forehead'. For me he is young, tall, wil-
lowy, fair, thoughtful, gay, with eyes like a fawn. He wears white
robes and carries a golden harp and his voice is like silver wind. He
would get on well with Gildas for they travelled together in the *Mabinogion*. A Breton legend has them as lifelong companions, the priest
and the Druid. He follows Gildas from Wales to Brittany and this is a
Christian legend so he later becomes a Christian. I'm sure old Gildas
kept pressing texts in his hand. Tradition has them buried in the
same abbey.

Henri broke one of his determined silences to tell me about life in
Douarnenez during the Hitler War, or at least Henri versus the SS. I
had often wondered what the German military men thought of the
Bretons for here would be a major collision of two conflicting
natures, the drivers and those who refused to be driven, the prosaic
versus the lyrical, worse, both nations were dreamers and there is
nothing more exasperating than another man's dream. It would be
the Saxons against the Celts all over again.

At first there was none of the gunpowder meeting fire that one
might expect. One of the more reliable of the madman Heinrich
Himmler's racial theories was that in Brittany was a pure ethnic
stock and they should be encouraged rather than put down, and even
the teaching of Breton at school was reintroduced. But then the
inmates of this ethnic menagerie started to bite. They blew up
bridges and a major part of the fishing community departed to Britain with their boats and joined General de Gaulle. The Germans felt
they had been let down.

In general those Bretons who stayed behind treated the occupying
power like one would a skin rash, making the best of it but hoping it
would go away. Anyway the troops in some rural areas were by no

means crack front line soldiers. They seemed to have spent most of their time trying to find something to eat, scouring the countryside for non-existent commodities like butter and eggs. At least they were non-existent as far as they could discover. Old *Jambe plastique* at Lervily, so called because arthritis made him walk as if he had an artificial leg, then a much younger man, actually threw one relentless scrounger into the midden to discourage his attentions. He was the hero of the hour and the village waited for the wrath to break over them, but nothing more was heard.

But it was a very different kind of soldier that young Henri saw glaring out of a wagon at him as he stood in the Douarnenez market trying to sell a few mackerel that the meagre petrol ration had allowed his father to catch. He was the biggest man Henri had ever seen, and it must be remembered that Henri was a very small one. The giant shouted something incomprehensible but Henri, guessing the import, affected not to hear. He heard the wagon door crash open and the next second he was lifted off the ground by his lapels.

'How much for the mackerel?' the giant shouted in bad French in Henri's face.

'Fifty francs,' stuttered the terrified Henri.

'Robber,' roared the giant, shaking Henri as a terrier would a rat.

'Five francs,' squealed Henri.

'Dot's better,' growled the giant. He set Henri down, stuffed the bank note in his top pocket, snatched the mackerel, and was gone.

Miserably Henri slunk away. Five francs was next to nothing, certainly not enough to pay for the fuel expended to catch the fish, not even for a loaf of bread. But looking at the note later Henri found that the giant had made a mistake. The note was not five, not fifty but five hundred francs, enough to keep the family in comparative luxury for a month.

We were now well into the region called Sizun which in Breton means 'seven days' and nobody seems to know why for it is a very strange name for a peninsula. I believe, but can't be sure, that term has something to do with the Druidical death ritual. The Druids believed that after death the soul had to pass through seven states of beatification before admittance to the Isle of the Blest, their Heaven. Maybe the cortège took a ritual seven days to pass through the area, with seven ceremonial stops overnight, the seventh on the headland of the Point du Raz. The old name for the island that lies off the headland means 'the isle of the seventh sleep'.

There's not much sleeping to be had here today. The tip of the Point has lately become infested with the boutiques of the tourist trash industry. Locronan has come to the majestic Beg ar Raz as it is called in Breton but with a certain nautical flavour for here you can buy desiccated starfish and spider crabs, varnished to make them look wet, wall ornaments such as plastic mermaids, plastic seagulls, glass net floats, and miniature crab and lobster pots at about ten times the price of the full sized ones. If you buy anything here, whether souvenir or refreshment, you will be afflicted with one of the most painful wasting diseases known to man — cirrhosis of the wallet.

But you can go beyond these temples to the gods of tourism and the pay telescopes, leave the wail of the canned bagpipe music behind, and find peace, that is almost peace for there are always shrieks from frightened tourists for the path over the slippery granite is far from safe and the safety rails are broken and corroded and not worth hanging on to. On either side there is a long drop and instant death. But if you survive it is worth the danger.

From the Beg you can look out across at least part of 'the angry sea', watch the cross-hatching of the fingers of current searching among the skerries and the coloured matchsticks of fishing boats vanishing between the shoulders of the swell. I thought of the months I spent out there with them and the sea is wild and seldom calm even in high summer.

You have to keep well clear of the draw of the rocks for they drag you on to them. One magical day it was calm and old Legrez took me into the middle of these stone icicles to prove there was nothing to it. We passed through foaming channels between barnacle encrusted rocks festooned with kelp and smelling like iodine on which razorbills and cormorants stood motionless like pterodactyls. Legrez (his name means 'lobster') had spent fifty years here and knew the ways of the sea. Not a breath of wind but even so his eyes were darting around looking for *an dri lam*, the third treacherous sea which the Bretons fear like the Devil's tongs. The trouble with the third wave is that it is equally likely to be second or fourth.

From the pinnacle above you can see the Isle of the Seventh Sleep or Sein as it called today. Here sea mists and fog banks are sudden and frequent. But the fact that the island is usually out of sight has little to do with poor visibility. Its average height above sea level is only three metres and even a moderate sea washes it from view. The island appears to be white and covered with lighthouses, one, they say, for each inhabitant. There are in fact about four hundred living on the island and only about five lighthouses on the 835 hectares of rock. The Senons are piratical and cruel semi-savages, that is when they are not being some of the warmest and most friendly people you've ever met. Most of the men understand English for they went to England with their boats when the Germans came.

Sein was a great Druid burial ground and they say it was also a Druid training college, not for men but for women. One of the principal priestess's names is recalled in another name for the island — 'the Isle of Velleda the Gaul'. Tradition says that here there was a great stone circle, very similar in looks and scale to Stonehenge but it was robbed of building material until nothing remained. This might be wishful thinking for according to prehistorians Stonehenge had nothing to do with the Druids, at least it was not built by them although they may have used it as a temple. But at such a distance it is difficult to be sure. Druidism did not come into being overnight and if other historians are to be believed there were kinds of Christians around long before Jesus Christ.

But that the island was a burial ground is reasonably certain for the bay opposite the island is called 'the Bay of the Dead'. Guide books will tell you that the bay got its name because after a shipwreck the drowned are washed up here. This is a fact but no more here than on any other inlet on this terrible coast. In fact the French translation of the Breton name '*boe an anaon*' is an incorrect one. 'Anaon' does not mean 'dead' but 'souls'. Local tradition says that here was the place of embarkment for Druid corpses for ferrying to the burial ground. There is a link here with Arthur.

The medieval romances have King Arthur and his knights questing the Holy Grail, either a chalice used at the Last Supper or in other versions the vessel in which Joseph of Arimathea caught the blood and tears of Jesus Christ. This is what they thought might be found at Glastonbury.

But according to the original Celtic legends this vessel was in another form. Arthur's men went looking for a cauldron called Annwn which was hidden somewhere across the seas. A great deal of mystery surrounds this quest for 'Annwn' which in Welsh legend is the Celtic Hades and there is doubt about the precise meaning of the word. Maybe the existence of the *boa an anoan* means we have stumbled across the answer to the riddle. Perhaps the quest is an allegory of life itself and that death, the finding of Anoan or Annwn, for the Breton and Welsh words are interchangeable, is the logical and inevitable outcome. Arthur and his men, whether they like it or not, will achieve a funerary urn in which their souls will at last repose in peace. They have reached the Otherworld. And most of them did in the legend of Annwn for not many of them came back of the three shiploads that went there.

I may have found Annwn but I lost my sunglasses. Walking across the sand toward the Hotel of the Bay of the Dead I was seized with the desire to play 'Ducks and Drakes'. I can skim a flat stone twenty times or more across reasonably flat water. When people are watching this is never more than seven times, or when I do succeed the audience insists that it wasn't watching. This has given rise to the charge that I am exaggerating. I suppose the violence of the throwing motion must have jerked the glasses from my pocket. Oddly enough the discovery of the loss threw Henri into a fit of hysterical laughter. He actually fell over and rolled on the sand. You can go off people.

The Bretons invariably find such things amusing. By nature they are frugal and they take immense care of personal possessions. I was forever losing knives over the side of my fishing boat, at least at first. But the Bretons do not leave things lying about but carefully put them away after use. Their watches are always secured by a piece of line about their necks. Consequently such losses are considered to be clownish behaviour and thought to be very funny. This is as close as I can get to an explanation of a Breton trait which sets them apart, which makes them 'different' and causes you to think again when you have decided that you know them inside out.

A manifestation of this trait can be extended to include a stalk of grass plucked while idling. The plucker will be holding the stalk in his hand sometimes hours after. It is not in the Breton nature to put things down without a positive decision to do so. The Bretons are so observant that they detected that I found this retention of a valueless piece of grass fascinating, although I had taken great care not to mention it or show it. At a later meeting the grass carrier would walk up to me, wink, tap me on the hand with the stalk then chuckle softly. This uncanny insight into one's thoughts is very disturbing.

I knew the hotel owners well. Before Clet and Marie-Jo' Brehonnet bought the derelict building they lived in the house up the road from me at Lervily. Clet was a cook on a cargo boat and I rarely saw him except for periods of home leave after four months at sea. Marie-

Jo' kept a boarding house for tourists, and still does for that matter. They had saved enough to buy the hotel and for Clet a life ashore.

He was one of the first to encourage me to speak Breton instead of French and used to roar with laughter at the results. I listened to his English and this had similar effect on me, for docks are not the most proper schools for the English language. But like most Breton chefs he can cook like a dream. Although I did have a bad meal at Chez Brehonnet on one occasion. This was at a wedding and I've eaten better in England. So if you want to dine well at the Bay of the Dead do it without the boisterous participation of three hundred Bretons.

I stayed the night at the hotel while Henri went off to find some relatives who lived nearby. He had a genius for nocturnal disappearances and morning manifestations in time for a liquid *petit déjeuner*. Maybe his relatives were the herring gulls or Arthur, Gildas and Taliesin. He never told me and I feared to ask him for this might be construed as an invitation to sleep at my expense.

The road south-west along the Baie d'Audierne to Lervily hugs close to the cliffs and unless there is flat calm and slack water is loud with the noise of the surf. There are no safe anchorages and *'porz'* means a windlass with a stout cable to drag small craft up a step ramp hewn out of the granite and a small ledge on which to perch nets and pots. Bestrée, a few kilometres from the Beg, is such a port and there are many like it either side of the peninsula.

Brittany is roughly divided by nomenclature into two parts. Inland is called 'ar goet' or 'the forest' and that dominated by the sea 'ar mor'. This last description was adopted and used by the Romans to describe the whole of Brittany. They called it Armorica — 'the land of the sea'. Nothing could be more apt for you can't escape it. The long Atlantic fetch strikes the coast and it trembles. It is a damp country and not an inch of granite is free from lichen, nor many old joints from arthritis.

One of the loveliest and loneliest of the many small cliff chapels is dedicated to Saint They. It is a plain oblong of dressed granite blocks with an open bell tower on the landward end. The angelus is rung by climbing the steps on the outside of the gable. In keeping with the dream quality of Brittany Saint They, or rather Saint Billy — for almost unbelievably they are the same corrupted by time, was never a hermit but a pebble. I found this out from an old lady of my village who was generally thought to be touched in the head.

Te-te Rose — Te-te is aunt in Brittany where all old people are called aunt or uncle out of respect — had the weathered brown complexion of most old Breton womenfolk, and a sad dignity of expression which worried you. But her smile would spread over her face like wind blowing across grass, a smile of such pure happiness that whenever I'd been away I used to seek her out just to see her smile so I knew I was home again.

Rose, like the other older women of the village, wore the kind of costume that should have been on our postcards. A small cap is held on the back of the head with hair clips. There is a white lace one for special occasions otherwise practically everything else that shows is as black as a winter storm. The hair is swept back from the face and secured under the cap in a bun, a masterpiece of stowage this for hanging loose it almost reaches to the waist.

A plain, high necked bodice disappears beneath a large silk apron, more of an overskirt, mostly black, but sometimes faintly striped in white or purple. Under this the skirt reaches down to mid-calf. This fullness above, black stockings, and the cumbersome plain wooden clogs below does wonders for the thickest old legs, making them appear slender, and importing a girlish quality to the walk of even very old women.

I must tell you about the ash clogs because from the very first they fascinated me, making me wonder why in an age of light footwear the Bretons hung on to them and refused to wear anything else. I've tried them and they are not for me. They are unpliant and my first few steps were nearly my last for I fell over. You require a peculiar gait to walk in them successfully and this requires a lifetime's usage.

The first thing that strikes you as queer is the toe which sweeps up to a beak. This was a mystery until I saw the fisherman hook them into the wooden lattice of the drum-shaped crab pots, to rebait them. The pots just rolled over rubber boots. Worn inside the clogs to protect the feet from the chafe and to keep them warm are woollen carpet slippers with felt soles. In the old days they used to stuff the clogs with straw but you seldom see this now. In very dry weather these inner slippers are worn without the clogs and being of wool and felt are washable. Clogs are never worn in the house and are left by the door.

In hot weather the clogs heat the feet like furnaces and the remedy is bathing the feet in sea water. Salt water is considered to be a cure-all on the Breton coast, footwash, antiseptic, eyewash and gargle all in one. Someone told me that he had seen drowned men thrown back into the sea in the hope that they might revive, but the man was a wag.

It was during one of her foot-bathing sessions that Te-te Rose told me about the magic of the pebbles or 'billies' as they are called in Breton.

'Listen to them now,' she said, and I listened. As the beds of billies rattled in the sink and drew off the surf they seemed to be chattering away like old ladies at a christening. The old people, Rose told me, listened to the voices of the pebbles and in time came to understand their language. They spoke of times to come, picked lovers, made decisions and told of life and death. To the earlier Bretons they were gods even. That Saint They was a 'Christianizing' of the billies is sure for the granite figure at the gate in the church wall has a pebble in the palm of one of his outstretched hands.

I asked Te-te Rose if she believed in the power of the billies to tell fortunes. There was that smile and a strange look in the small eyes. 'If you want to believe, you will believe,' she said in her flute voice. The billies had told her that her husband would never come home. She hadn't believed the billies because the weather had been calm for days and she had already seen him bring his boat alongside the quay and come ashore safely. She had climbed the hill to prepare his supper, leaving him to arrange the warps for the rise and fall of the tide. Later they came to tell her that her husband had gone to the bistro, then back to the boat to see all was well. He had fallen off the quay and drowned for the Bretons are not swimmers. They had carried the body to the house of their son where it lay until the funeral two days later.

I was sad for Rose but she said that it had happened a long time ago and she no longer thought about him, but she had loved her husband for he was a good man and a fine fisherman and they had been young at the time. I asked Rose if she would listen to see if the billies spoke about me. She said she would but I must leave her alone. She never mentioned the billies when I saw her next and maybe she had forgotten. By then I had made my voyages on the tunnyman and come home safely so I no longer cared so much what the billies might say.

Writing this far from Brittany this story seems weird to me now but I did not doubt the power of the billies at the time. And not too long ago my village was callled not Lervily but Kerbilly, 'the village of the talking stones' so we weren't the only believers by a long way.

Henri and I and my mythical companions climbed a small coombe and came into the granite village of Plogoff, just a few houses, a general store, and a very large church. Most churches in Brittany have a stele near the porch, a single granite column tapered towards the top and perhaps two metres high, sometimes decorated with fluting, sometimes left plain. The steles marked a Druid meeting place and the Christians built their churches next to them or moved them into the churchyard so as not to risk the congregation preferring the stele to the pulpit.

The church of Saint Ké at Plogoff has a very elegant stele. Some see it as a phallic symbol, but some see a phallus in wine bottles. Ké was supposed to have been an Irish monk who led his flock to Brittany to escape the Saxons, but there is another belief about this hermit. Ké appeared in the legends as Keu and the romances as Sir Kay and was a member of the Round Table and one of King Arthur's favourite knights or followers. After the death of Arthur at Camlann he forsook the sword and became a monk, later an archbishop in Britain then one in Brittany. That's what they say locally.

A road leading off to the right takes you to Killiwic or Quillivic according to the French cartographers. This was one of Arthur's strongholds in the legends, possibly a hill fort. But there isn't a fort on the hill here, and no sign that there ever has been one, only a small chapel with a plain wooden ceiling and by the altar a collection of Celtic saints, carved in wood with strange Tartar eyes, model sailing vessels fitted with poles so that they could be carried at religious processions called 'Pardons', and a pile of hymnals in Breton. I'd never seen this before. But there are quite a few Kelliwics in Brittany's Cornwall and I might not have been at the right one.

At first I used to examine the faces of my fellow villagers and wonder what it was that was so peculiar about them, why they did not at all resemble Frenchmen. Then I saw that they had the same kind of eyes that you see in the faces of old wooden and granite figures. This feature ranges from a barely perceptible downward slope of the brows to wedge shaped orbits that would not look out of place in one of Genghiz Khan's horsemen.

The Celts are supposed to have commenced their migration westward from southern Germany and Bohemia, finally dominating the whole of Europe from the Rhine to Ireland. Much later the Bretons made a reverse migration from Britain to populate Armorica. This is accepted opinion but oddly enough the Bretons have no folk

memory, tradition or legend about this migration or their origin in
the British Isles, very strange in a people who speak of happenings of
centuries ago as if they had taken place last week. To the contrary
they say they came not from the west but the east, but in saying so
they think they must be wrong for their schooling tells them otherwise. To my mind there is more than a chance that the Bretons may
be right and the historians wrong.

The main argument against the supposition is of course the might
of ecclesiastical history. The Bretons have no written evidence that
says otherwise. But there is something queer about this migration of
a beaten people to Gaul in direct competition with the fierce Franks
who themselves were thrusting in the opposite direction. Another historical trump card is the similarity of Breton place names with those
in Britain, postulating that the emigrants took them with them, not
only towns and villages but kingdoms like Dumnonia and Kernow,
the old names for Devon and Cornwall. As it later happened in America it had happened in Brittany. And had not the actual name of the
country 'Brittany' been taken from its original Britain? Obvious con-
clusions are sometimes treacherous and a little sober reflection suggests that it did not. In fact it is more likely that the opposite is the
case.

Before Caesar took his army across the English Channel earlier historians were calling the British Isles not Britain but the Pretanic
Isles. Its inhabitants were called the Pretanii coming from the Celtic
meaning 'the painted ones'. Scholastic Julius had encountered in
Gaul a Belgic tribe somewhere south of Boulogne, we can't be precise, called the Britanii. Hearing that a Belgic tribe had migrated
across the Channel sometime earlier he thought he was correcting an
error when he started calling the people that gave him such a hot
reception when he came ashore from his galleys the Britanii and their
island Britannia. In fact it was he who was making the error.

Even the duplication of place names theory is suspect. Let's take
for example the kingdom of King Maelgwn, the two Gwenydds, one
in Wales and the other in Brittany, where my friend Taliesin made
the old bards go 'bleroom . . . bleroom'. It is supposed that Welsh
migrants to Brittany took the name with them, another obvious conclusion. This is nonsense.

Armorica's most fractious tribe although known as the Venetii to
the Romans actually called themselves something like the 'Gwendawti', meaning 'the white ones', and their tribal territory 'Gwened'.

They had done so before the Romans came to Gaul, and many, many centuries before the Saxons invaded Britain.

Nevertheless British archaeologists would have us believe that a tribe found a land already named for itself between the third and sixth centuries of this era. This would be similar to a tribe, say called the Mancunians or the Brooklyners who for no other reason than caprice took off across the seas and found a place already called Manchester or Brooklyn. I am not prepared to believe this.

But there can't be much doubt that during that period a large number of Celtic monks were travelling to Brittany. And it seems that a large number of Roman monks, Saint Augustine among them, were arriving in Britain to evangelize the Saxons. That the Celts had made no steps in this direction was bewailed by the new arrivals but with an air of piousness which is suspect. It is likely that the migration to Brittany was no more than an ecclesiastical one, that the story of the migration of the populace of Britain was a piece of Church propaganda to explain in the nicest possible way the conflict between the long hairs and the tonsures.

People were far more unstickable in those days than we can really appreciate. We now have a roll on, roll off mentality but there are families in my village who have never been further than the Audierne market. The old Celtic population of Britain would have thought long and hard before wandering off from the comparative safety of their native heath, especially when they could not be sure that they wouldn't meet Saxons on the road. Not much more than two centuries have passed since a winter's journey from London to Brighton was considered too impracticable, not just because of footpads but because the road was impassable. It was the invention of macadam surfaces that made even the summer journey less than a triumph of endurance.

Just before Lervily stands the church of Saint Tujen, the scourge of rabid dogs and toothache, for the lead keys they sell there have the remarkable power of slaying one and curing the other. Some say that Tujen came from what we now call England, others say Wales, anyway he came with the stone trough armada sometime in the sixth century. The site was another old Druid meeting place and the altar is said to be part of the capstone of a dolmen. But how the experts can guess that this ultimate in Christian vandalism is such is beyond me for as in the case of alligators one flat stone is very like the next.

It seems that the Celtic monks loved their sisters very much, for

Tujen, and the story is repeated endlessly for other holy arrivals from Britain, brought her with him. For the old chroniclers, no doubt glorifying the works of the Lord, these young women are always beautiful, which might give the wrong idea about the relationship. And these ladies always seem to become pregnant and how this happens is always attributable to the cunning of the existing population, presumably the Gauls.

Miss Tujen's downfall was due to the failure of a test thought up by the saint to see whether lusty men were hiding in the long grass close to his hermitage. He threw stones into the underbrush and if birds flew out in alarm then he knew it was free of humanity. But some genius conceived the idea of letting caged birds escape when the stones fell amongst them. Satisfied by the ruse she went to the pool, stripped off, and the Gauls satisfied her even more. This must have made Tujen sorry that he had got rid of all the mad dogs for one of these let loose in the bushes would have acted as a powerful contraceptive.

Henri said that he wanted to see a local peasant about some work and this suited my purpose for I wanted to return to Lervily on my own. Arthur and the others could be switched off when I didn't need them. I never saw Henri again. He strolled out of my life in the same casual way as he had entered it at Arzal.

My village is draped over the summit of a hill but as it was built by fishermen the cottages are hidden from the gales in hollows and face south and the winter sun as if aligned by compass. Cities are small enough for towns in Brittany and so on down the scale so Lervily is only a hamlet but there was a time when the harbour had as many as fifty sail. Now there is only one fishing boat and soon she will be gone.

Lervily is dying of medicine, from pensions and early retirement from the sea. In the bad old days death came early and made room for the next generation. Now Lervily, like many similar villages, is a kind of open geriatric ward, and the young fishermen have moved away to where there is space for new houses. So although the fishing industry still flourishes it does so from the other side of the Gwaien, from the cement block houses which are spreading up the river valley. The boats are larger and use the more convenient and safer port of Audierne.

Saint Edwette, the port of Lervily, was always a precarious roost, unsafe from September to May, surviving by sheer cussedness and

the fact that Audierne dried out. It offered very little shelter at all.
Just after the Hitler War a great concrete mole was built to help matters but this merely succeeded in altering the scour of the tides and
the old quay was suffocated to death by sand banks.

A new quay was built close to the mole where the water was still
deep enough to accommodate the boats. But Saint Edwette was
dying anyway. Engines were replacing sails and these gave a permanent fair wind up to the Audierne where there was a market. If there
was water enough the boat did not hang about in Saint Edwette any
more.

But the sand banks were a blessing in disguise for Lervily. The
same sand which choked Saint Edwette in time grew to form a vast
beach, ideal for buckets and spades, bikinis, and the sale of ice
cream. For the two months of the summer when hot sun can be relied
on the sand is covered with them. Then with the first breath of winter
in September Saint Edwette dies and it is lonelier than it has ever
been.

The path from the Beg is lit by the golden fire of gorse and the purple milk of heather. On your right is the sea with great granite blocks
flashing with mica. On your other hand is a low horizon, sea pasture
divided by granite walls, miles of them, making us wonder at the
work which went into them. But they were built by carrying a few
rocks at a time up from the shore. The men who started them saw no
completion during their lifetime.

It is a land of herring gulls and vipers and lizards, cormorants,
migrant whimbrels and kittiwakes and starlings searching for grubs
in the great banks of kelp formed over the billies. The tourists draw
deep breaths of what they think is ozone. It is in fact the smell of rot-
ting seaweed and dead fish, but it does them good all the same. Here
the old villagers search for limpets and trap starlings in nooses of fine
line. They no longer need such food for survival but they do it
because they have always done so. I find limpets rubbery but the old
ones say I am too fastidious, that there is nothing better than a limpet
scooped fresh from the shell and eaten with a hunk of black bread
and a cup of rough red wine. They call them 'Lervily oysters' and
chuckle when the tourists look the other way. But strangers always
look the other way when Bretons eat because they have a horrifying
way with the pointed blades of pocket knives with which they thrust
food down their throats, the thumb acting as a clamp.

Up along the lighthouse at Pen ar ros and you come into the vil-

lage by Tante'phine's, a rough triangle of a square lined by granite
cottages with slate roofs covered with lichen. The courtyards are
trodden mud where you see crab pots and nets hanging to dry on the
walls.

Lervily, like the people, or because of them, has moods. It can
appear deserted or busy, for villages have times for doing things. It is
the hour or not the hour for this or that. For a people with little clock
sense they are remarkably predictable when you get to know them.
But try to nail them down to keeping an appointment at a certain
hour and they become uncomfortable and evasive. Any prearrange-
ment will not be kept, but they will drift up eventually in their own
good time without any apology for the fact that you have marching
the quay, dashing out cigarettes and looking at your watch in frustration. It is your fault because you set the time, not they.

Even when I was working regularly with a crab boat there was not
one occasion when I was told a precise time for going to sea.

'What time tomorrow?' I used to ask.

'In the morning,' came the reply.

'I know that, but at what time?'

There would be the shrugging of shoulders and gasps of exaspera-
tion. I learned that 'in the morning' meant sometime about dawn.
Dawn has quite a lot of latitude between dark and first light but they
would all turn up at the same time although coming from different
ends of the village.

Eventually I never needed an alarm clock. The heartbeat of Lervily began to control me. I awoke naturally, dressed, drank my bowl
of coffee and milk, then wandered down to the quay. I would meet
the others on the way. Sometimes when the weather was bad I would
wake and listen to the wind then go back to sleep again. I became a
nice judge of sea conditions in a way I cannot explain. It could be
entirely due to the sound of the wind on the roof for gales are as freak-
ish as their effect on the sea. In time I developed 'instinct' and if I was
mistaken I knew I would hear an angry clog against the door. This on
occasion happened to us all, mainly after a late night. So Lervily has
no clock but a natural pulse dictated by custom and an admixture of
mood. But I can approximate.

Eight o'clock, morning, is the stacatto hour of clogs, the trundling
of wheelbarrows, women to Tante'phine's to purchase groceries and
order bread, brief visits these for there is no time for other than
urgent gossip, for the cottage must be cleaned and bed linen thrown

out over the window sill to air. The old retired fishermen are marching down the hill to the other bistro about a kilometre along the coast
road to Audierne. Tante'phine sells wine but the men can't stand the
looks from the women and seek the peace of the Pouldhu. The wheelbarrows of laundry are off to the *lavoir*, for gossip to soapsuds and
scrubbing brushes. By nine the square is empty again and Tante-
'phine's is silent apart from the roar of the oven. The first batch of
black bread delicious enough to make you yearn for the taste will be
ready at ten o'clock and the women come back for prolonged gossip
and the men will be tramping back up the hill.

Just after eleven o'clock the black of the women will be changed to
the faded patched blue cotton of the men. By mutual consent the two
streams never mix, black out, blue in. Eleven is the hour of the aperitif and no woman dare stand in the way of that. For the old male
Breton the aperitif is a prolongation of the morning glass of wine,
but it is a right all the same. It is also the hour of travellers from the
other villages such as Youenn the Post and Fanchic the Fruit with
news which must not be missed. Some of the men do work in their
gardens but this is not demanding and they can fit in the growing of
vegetables with filling their bloodstreams full of alcohol, talking
about the movements of the fishing boats, the price of fish and how
times used to be, and how Brittany is heading for disaster under the
present regime in Paris.

By 'kreistez' — meaning both 'noon' and 'due south' because at
midday that is where the sun lies — all Lervily is quiet again. The families are eating their boiled potatoes and fish. Meat is not thought
much of on the coast. It is fine for Sundays but once a week is
enough, too much for some, for fish eating constitutions can't stand
the chemistry. Cold meat is a kind of poison and the reason why restaurants serve it under the name of *assiette anglaise*. English carni-
vores are considered to be reckless with their livers. The French talk
about their livers as the English do their heads, purging them with
bottled mineral water, just as we seek respite with aspirin.

After a siesta the men are driven into the vegetable plots if they
can't plead bad weather. If it is raining they work in outhouses mend-
ing the fishing nets of the tourists. This is much better for they are out
of sight and they can wander off without detection, and if their
absence is discovered they had to go and get some twine from a neighbour, who has also gone to get some from another. This excuse is
never believed but it has great scope for belief and if they have

scrounged a fish or two from one of the boats at the quay then the absentees are forgiven.

By five o'clock a litre of wine becomes official and the women can be stared back at or just ignored. And there is a bench along the sunny wall at the other side of the square. After all they could have been there all the time and the fact they were in the café when the wife came in coincided with an attack of thirst.

Even in a nation of heavy drinkers — the latest figure I've seen is 106.4 litres of wine per head per annum, man, woman and child — the average Breton is considered a heavy drinker. The casualty rate is high and there are many special hospitals for crabs in the head. But otherwise the Breton is a drinker as opposed to a drunkard. Drinking is the Celtic disease and it does them no good. The Breton is naturally gay and garrulous and an entertainer but alcohol makes him as dull, repetitive and melancholy as any Saxon. Old Fayot is one of the most interesting talkers I yet have met but a few glasses too many poses in his mind the kind of question which has vexed the philosophers down the ages.

'Just what are we doing here?' he will demand of the assembly. 'Are we some kind of ant?'

He shoots a murderous glance up at the ceiling. 'What does he think he's doing with us? That's if there *is* anyone up there. *Bullharst*, I don't believe that nonsense for a moment. I'm not to be taken in by priests who live off old women and poor idiots.' Nobody has said a word or moved hand or head.

Tante'phine is God's representative in her bistro and such blasphemy is likely to get the bottle removed from the table but Fayot will vociferously fly into the flame like a moth. This is living dangerously and the Celt loves it. An attempt to change the subject will result in even more anger, agreement with the theme is equally dangerous. It is time to leave. Fayot will charge through us, elbowing his way first to the door. This is to give the impression that he was going anyway, indeed it was he who wanted to leave not us. Multiply Fayot by the dozen and you have Lervily, and Lervily by the thousand and you have Brittany. By eight o'clock the bistro will be empty, by nine the village is in bed, if not asleep.

Lervily is a generalization and so is Fayot and to generalize about Bretons is to generalize about Africans or Americans. They wear the same cotton smock and trousers and a blue navy cap. This is a generalization. They just appear to do so. Fayot is typical but he

wears a beret. So does old Jean Jauoin. They all wear clogs but
Fayot sometimes wears rubber-soled leather boots with an elastic
band over the hooks instead of laces. They all wear Breton navy blue
sweaters under their smocks but Fayot wears a black polo-necked
jumper under a blue overall jacket. The obvious conclusion is that
Fayot is different. They are all different. But they do different things
in the same way. So Fayot is typical although he is different.

Another peculiarity which damages my theory about the existence
of a typical Breton is that even if you see him at a distance you know
who it is. The outline is the same but just as you can tell a man from a
woman at a distance by the way they move, I can tell Josée from Youenn ar braz, Théophile from old Daniel, and a stranger from anyone
else because his movements are unfamiliar.

Youenn ar braz skates on imaginary ice with his hands behind his
back, rhythmically sliding each clog forward. Old Daniel's legs seem
somehow connected to his elbows and he flaps them like a frantic
albatross. Théophile has hairs up his nostrils and as he rolls along he
punishes the irritation with the back of his right hand. Charles is a
swift moving shoulder roller, who knew I was interested in such
things and said I walked like a tiger with a broken neck. His demonstration was disturbing.

The Breton is an excellent mimic and I've seen one exactly imitate
another so as we knew who we were talking about entirely without
rehearsal. I believe this is due to an innate ability for noticing detail.
Watch a Breton crew cleaning a net, eyes not only checking the mesh
for tears but continually watching the strain on a boat's mooring
warps. Things have a habit of going wrong swiftly at sea and this constant vigilance keeps him alive longer.

So a Breton naturally notices the colour of your handkerchief and
the way you lace your boots. And just as a dog knows when his master is going for a walk instead of popping outside for something, the
Breton sees things that others have lost the art of seeing. He is a fine
judge of mood. Preoccupied with some problem I would enter Tante-
'phine's and the conversation would fall silent immediately, or die to
whispers. In another mood I would have been greeted with hand-
shakes and banter. So Lervily is not a good place to be jollied out of
ill humour. The change must come from within for sadness seems to
be contagious and it poisons the atmosphere.

I walked quickly through the village just after nine o'clock so I saw
nobody. I wanted it that way, but I was sure I was being watched for

no-one enters or leaves the village without being seen. Turning right I descended the narrow track to my old cottage, past the house of an old fisherman whom I have never met.

There are not a few fishermen like that in Lervily and some you only see rarely, on a fine day dozing in a chair in the courtyard. Arthritis in some degree comes to all the old fishermen in such a damp climate. He has to keep moving for as long as he can. Only by exercise can he delay the inevitable. When he is no longer able to walk he takes to his bed to await the next inevitability. And he will wait, perhaps, for many years for immobility does not tax the heart. So except for the immediate family death is not such a sad occasion as it is elsewhere. The coffin bearers may not for many years have spoken to the man they carry to the cemetery up the hill. I've attended sadder weddings in Britain.

There are no professional undertakers nearer than Quimper so we dispose of the dead ourselves. It is a cottage industry. I had lived in the village five years before the summons eventually came. It was not the first death in the village during my tenure but until then I had been a stranger and for the Bretons death is a private matter.

It was a dark, gusty November evening when I received the summons. Lannic stood in the rain, his face sombre under a new cap.

'Old Clet is dead,' he said. Like this other neighbour I had never met Clet. But I knew the widow, a great, boisterous old lady who spent so much time occupied with my affairs and with such persistence that I constructed a kind of aeroplane out of packing cases and planks in the yard just to see her eyes fly up into her lace coif.

'But I don't know Clet,' I protested. I wanted to avoid the formal visit paid to the corpse, and the sunken faces of the old ladies seated on benches in the death chamber. I told Lannic so.

'More than that. You are chief undertaker,' said Lannic. 'Come with me.'

I was escorted not to the widow's house but to Tante'phine's. It was brilliantly lit like a lighthouse in the dark village and despite the lateness of the hour packed to the doors. There was much wine drinking but my ordeal was to come, and it was described to me with such attention to detail it produced a feeling akin to panic.

Had I shaved a corpse before? Pity, but it wasn't too difficult if I managed to prise open the stiff jaws and push out the cheeks with a forefinger. I protested frantically that I didn't own a razor. I was told not to worry on that score as no doubt the dead man had one that he wouldn't be using. They were sure that I had soap and that would be needed to cleanse the body. And a sponge, surely I had a sponge?

Then the body would have to be plugged. Plugged? Surely I had heard of body juices? Then I was to dress the corpse in a clean shirt and collar and black tie and twist a rosary into the dead hands. It was easy when you knew how and now we had a hideous pantomime with José with body tensed playing the part of the deceased. My trembling hand produced a froth on the wine so they thought I'd better have a rum before going to the widow's house.

'What are you lot going to do then?' I cried in desperation. There was a general shaking of heads. They would have loved to have helped me but as nearest neighbour I had to do it all alone. It was the custom.

We trooped out of Tante'phine's and the others went off home leaving Lannic to conduct me to my fate. He held my arm in a strong grip to see that I did not escape, an act which I was contemplating. When we got to my cottage he let out a powerful chuckle and gave me a shove which nearly sent me head first down the steps. It had all been a joke — ha-ha. The services described to me had already been performed by the women. All I had to do was to help put the corpse in the coffin on the morrow. I was to be 'bifstek' — muscle and nothing more — ho-ho. And screw the lid down and carry the coffin about — he-he. Even so I didn't sleep very well.

The taxi arrived from the shipwrights with the coffin and then the rector flicked bottled mineral water over Old Clet and ordered me to do the same. I wondered whether it would be appropriate as a Protestant but the rector said I must. So the old mariner went into his box damp with spray like he had passed most of his life. He was very heavy, Old Clet, but we got him in and screwed down at last. After the service in the church at Esquibien we pushed him to the church yard on a trolley with large spoked wheels known locally as the curé's bicycle. 'I thought for a moment I was off for a ride on the curé's bicycle,' we used to say after a trawl wire had parted and whistled close to our heads and gouged a gash in the deck instead.

There was a great deal of shoving to get at the religious ornaments to carry in the procession to the cemetery. The object was to avoid carrying one of the two great wax candles for these attracted vulgar jokes because of their similarity to male sexual organs. After this was over the bearers and the close relatives went to a nearby restaurant for a light meal and drinks paid for by the widow. Imprisoned in suits and tight collars we made the best of it with anecdotes. Old Clet was already on his way to the Isle of the Wind and already seemed forgotten.

My cottage lies in a small hollow in the side of the hill which runs down to the sea shore and is protected on all sides from the wind except to the south west. From the bank above you can see clear across the Baie d'Audierne to Penmarc'h, across the rock shoal called ar Gambole where even on calm days the breakers roar into the river mouth, each sea trailing a white plume like a Roman charioteer. You can feel the tremble at the cottage and hear the mournful honk of the buoy marking the west side of the reef. This noise dominates Lervily, and I shall never forget it.

From this bank my wife had seen my tunnyman cross the rim of the sea after her voyage to the Azores and put a line on to a buoy in Saint Edwette harbour for the last time. I had lost over a stone in weight, grown several years older in just a few months, had three fractured ribs, bruised thighs, lacerated hands, and had learned to love the land and fear the sea. As I wrote then for a time my life was intensified until I wanted no more of it. For many nights after I lay awake revelling in the comfort and thought of *Jacques et René* and the glow of her navigation lights, damp, cold, smelling of dank iron, rolling through the night. And I vowed that nothing would induce me to take up such a challenge again.

But the cottage was mine no longer and there was long grass and ferns where Mary-Louise had laboured in the hot sun to produce our year's supply of vegetables. I thought of the countless number of barrowfuls of seaweed I had pushed up the hill to enrich the thin soil. We had dug and weeded the earth until it was clean. But now only a few months later the ground was as choked and overgrown as it had been when we had bought the empty cottage.

Like the chapels, Breton cottages are simple oblongs of granite blocks built on a granite outcrop. Between the end gables the oblong was built up to about three metres and levelled off with stone flags. To this was spiked a wooden beam into which were slotted the rafters. Formerly the roof was thatched and the sculptured corbels to contain the thatch were still there, standing above the present plank and slate roof. Into the inside faces of the walls were fitted pine beams to support the planked ceiling which was also the floor of the garret.

The interior was divided into one large and one small room by a wooden walled passage which acted as a wind trap and a hanging space for oilskins and a clog park. The door and the two windows, one to each room, facing south, were the only breaks in the thick walls, apart from a small niche housing a Virgin and Child so they could be seen from inside and out.

The cottages never have inside lavatories but one in an outhouse. The idea of sanitary plumbing is considered to be foolhardy and the daily ritual of the bucket with each row of vegetables favoured in strict rotation is as Breton as the lace coif itself, but as a pastorale has so far been neglected by illustrators of picture postcards. Far from being envious of inside lavatories old Jean Jauoin was horrified by the disgusting habits he'd discovered during a visit to his son-in-law's house at Paris:

'Filthy, disgusting,' he said. 'They actually shit inside their houses.'

I waded through the weeds which was once Mary-Louise's flower garden and sought for the key in its hiding place under a stone near the door. It was still there. I unlocked the door and entered. There was a smell of dank wood and damp stone. And of wood smoke from the ingle nook in the main room and perhaps some of the essence of the paraffin lamps but I could be dreaming.

Between the stone shoulder of the ingle nook and the wall was where I used to prop myself to play my accordian for I loved the accoustics — 'Dusty's Corner' it was called. The chamber was empty now but to my right used to be the great table where we ate and drank for hours on end. And there was the stone floor where Emile the Plumber danced with Alain the Fisherman in the hop and shuffle but laughing all the time. And by the door stood Big Charles roaring songs in a voice which knew no musical scale, but all the same we loved them for their volume and enthusiasm. It was a style of singing he must have preferred for one evening he sang a song as tunefully as you could wish. Overcome we asked him what he was up to. He replied that the song was an old one of his grandfather's and he always sang it like that.

We all sang. The Bretons are enthusiastic singers during meals, between courses, the women as well as the men, each taking turn and each being kissed as a reward by the other sex. These meals lasted all evening and well into the early hours of the morning. Everyone had brought along something to eat so it didn't cost much. The men brought wine, the women a cake, and there was fish from the boats, a lobster too sometimes. Mussels scraped from the underside of the

Gambole buoy, shrimps caught in small pots, watercress from the river, and oysters scrounged from somewhere.

I stood in the empty room hearing the voices just as they had been. I had also slept in that room when I came home from the sea when it was too hot in the garret upstairs, and I had written in it too while wood lice dropped on my head. In the winter we had such fires, great fires of driftwood which sometimes set fire to the soot up the chimney so we had to drench it with water. I could still hear the roof drumming with the winter gales and rafters grinding in their sockets. And one day after weeks of heavy rain from the ingle nook had burst a spring which shot through the room and poured out of the door. But I had been at sea and Mary-Louise had suffered alone.

It was, perhaps this suffering alone which made me lose her. She spoke fluent French, I preferred to stumble along in Breton. Our worlds were different. I had my fishermen, she had the shopkeepers to whose children she gave English lessons. To me her kind seemed fatuous and false. My kind she could not understand. Apart from Alain she never got to know them for they are shy and awkward in other company and they avoid it. We grew apart until one could not hear the other any more.

I locked the door for the last time and put the key back under the stone close to where the fire of the petunias still burned in my memory. This is where the hawk moths hovered and we looked forward to them coming each year. I ran up the steep stone steps to the narrow road, turned right to the coast road, past Lagrez's cottage with the collapsing roof mended with tin trays and canvas.

'Ho,' he roared from his window. But I could not, dare not turn back.

6 Bassas, City of the Legion, and Celidon

Wihtgar Hairybreeks put the steering oar hard over and his galley was the first to grind her keel on the gravel of the mighty river. The others came to the shore one by one resting on their oars, the great dragons of sixty oarsmen. The Saxons slid over the gunwales and into the edge of the still flooding tide, wading ashore with water to their waists. Spikes for the mooring were knocked into soft alluvium and the boats with their fierce dragon heads swung round to face the estuary mouth.

Then the exhausted men threw themselves down on the warm turf and were asleep. But Wihtgar was content for the while. He let them sleep, great warriors all of them with names of valour like Oslak Great Axe, Cynric Fork Beard and Stuf the Fart. They had made the great voyage and one of the richest prizes in Gaul lay before them, the city of Naoned.

Once Naoned had been called Condevicnum but the Romans had marched away. Now the guardians were mere Celts, fine enough warriors but squabblers and divided against themselves. Silver and gold plate, church ornaments, rings, cattle — and women, fiery and treacherous but good in the straw. Wihtgar rubbed his hands in anticipation. Yes, let them sleep his terrible wielders of the axe, let the ebb and flow pass again under the keels of his dragons for ahead lay a day's march to the treasure vaults.

After washing down a hunk of mutton with some wine and giving a final glance at the silent trees Wihtgar himself slept. The tide had turned and already the dragons were settling in the mud, resting over on to their broad bilges. Let them sleep too. They would not be wanted until the next flood tide awoke them again, when hull down with plunder the great oars would guide them out into the ebb and down the river to the open sea.

Wihtgar Hairybreeks was the first to die, a spear through his throat. With great blasts on war horns and terrible screams the Celts were amongst them. The forest was alive with them. At their head was Arthur, slashing with his great sword, Caliburn. He fought like a berserk, the sweat streaking the chalk on his face. He slew a half-dozen before they could raise themselves to their elbows. Keu, Bedwyr, Gwian, Lancelin, Tristram, blue war paint glistening, were at his shoulder and slew many more.

Arthur had waited for this moment. He had watched the dragons creeping towards the coast, then turn into the estuary, their flashing blades sweeping them into the river, saw them come ashore.

'Kill them now,' Lancelin had urged him. The great warrior had put his hand on his shoulder and shaken his head. Far better to wait until the ebb had left the dragons and made escape impossible — or the Saxons would return. Arthur never quite trusted Lancelin. His eyes were always on Gwenhwyvaer and hers on him. The chief took great care never to turn his back on the younger man. He would deal with him later but now they must wait.

The carnage had been total. None of the Saxons were allowed to live although they had screamed when they had been thrown with the dead on the funeral pyre, once their prized dragons. They would not be needing them any more. Arthur cleaned his spear on a tuft of grass. His men were whooping, drunk on captured wine and fighting for the spoil, bragging about their prowess in the fight. They had dyed the River Bassas red with Saxon blood. It had not always been that way but under Arthur they had fought back, at Glein, four times at Dubglas, and now here.

Then a drove of screaming children jumped from the Citroën and assaulted the Coca-Cola machine and the *madame* at the service station screamed at them:

'*Vous avez des pièces*?' And Arthur and his men dashed for cover and the vision dissolved like a paper hat in a rain storm. This was a shame for I'd searched quite some time for the site of Arthur's sixth battle.

There is no such word as 'Bassas' in the Old Welsh in which Nennius wrote his History. Opinion has been strong that 'Bas' meant 'shallow' and that the rest of the word had been a case of dittography for when translating British words into Latin the monks were prone to adding senseless syllables, either to show off or to break the monotony.

As far as I could discover there was neither a river called 'Bassas'

nor the more intelligible 'Bas' in Brittany. There is an island on the
north coast near Roscoff called Enez Batz but Nennius had written
of a river, 'on the river Bassas' to be precise. I wondered if the word
could have been completely Latin and something to do with 'bass' or
'lower'. I couldn't find anything like it except for one meaning 'kiss'
and this is hardly likely. This had got me nowhere but I was on the
right track.

The Loire is the lowest or most southerly river in Brittany. The
name comes from the Roman Liger Fluvius and it divided the old
Roman provinces of Aquitania and Gallia Lugdunensis. It is the
longest river in France, commencing a thousand kilometres away in
that great spine of France, the Massif Central. There have always
been battles fought on or around this river. The Romans had
brought their Mediterranean galleys here by wagon and packhorse,
reassembled them and sailed out to fight the warships of the Venetii.
Later in A.D. 843 a great fleet of longships had sailed up the river to
Naoned, now Nantes, and the Norsemen had decapitated the archbishop. Saint Gohard, however, had put them to flight by appearing
at the door of his cathedral with his crosier in one hand and his head
in the other.

But had the river ever been connected with 'Bas'? There is much evidence that it has. An island in the Loire estuary was called 'Baf' or
'Bas' until the ninth century. The town of Batz at the river mouth on
the northern bank was also called 'Baf', 'Bas', or 'Bath'. So the Loire
could have been called 'Bas' or Nennius's 'Bassas' after all.

But for historical daydreaming about Arthur the Bas of today is a
lead balloon. The great naval dockyard of Saint Nazaire stretches
for ten kilometres up one bank and Saint Brevin does the same for
the other. And at Batz itself, possibly the site of Arthur's battle, you
are more likely to get a lollipop stuck in your throat than a spear.

Not far away is the great French holiday prison of La Baulle and
all the inmates come to Batz to see the famous cross which is supposed to cure rheumatism. It is a disppointment, like finding that the
Eiffel Tower is only a few centimetres high. The cross, a 'Christianized' menhir, is set in a wall between 22 and 24 rue de la Gare. You
have to rub the affected part against the stone and say a *pater noster*
and an *avé*, a cure guaranteed within seven days or your skin back.

I asked a gendarme who was standing near by, twisting his moustache and regarding my red tennis shoes with hatred, if the stone
really worked.

'But yes, *monsieur*,' he replied. 'Only the other day a drunken Englishman ran his head against the stone and will never suffer with rheumatism again.' I had never encountered a gendarme with a sense of humour and told him so. He must have been one of those straight-faced comedians for he turned on his heel and stalked away without another word.

My tennis shoes were badly broken and made a strange sound with every footstep so I bought another pair as a souvenir of Batz. Old shoes have a strange power. Unlike anything else you can't just throw them in a dustbin. You have to do it by stealth. While doing so when I thought nobody looking I heard a clatter of boots and found the comic gendarme watching me over my shoulder. When I looked back he was shaking them free of refuse and he went off with them under his arm. I suppose that when I am eventually arraigned before a tribunal as an enemy of the Republique they will be produced as evidence.

Nantes is as attractive a city as you'll find anywhere, mostly medieval and tastefully modern and built about the great château of Anne de Bretagne — 'the duchess in clogs' — who in 1499 married wily King Louis, achieving in the bedchamber what centuries of bloody warfare had failed to do, the unification of France with Brittany.

The Bretons don't consider the Nantais to be real Bretons, particularly those who live south of the Loire. They call them 'cabbages', a mild enough insult but still dangerous in a proud university city. They grow them there in some quantity. It is also the centre of the area which produces Muscadet, the only wine which can be said to be Breton. If a pearl had a taste it would taste like good Muscadet. Drink it cool but not chilled with shellfish and you have a banquet. But don't drink the red. It's cheap enough, perhaps only two or three francs a bottle, but it won't keep, quickly degenerating to rusty latchkeys which plait your teeth.

I told a waiter so and made him angry.

'You don't know good wine, monsieur,' he said. I agreed but added that I knew bad wine, God knows I'd drunk enough of the stuff, and the sample before us was a fine example of it. I would take a glass of cider instead. After keeping me waiting an hour or so he came back to say that he couldn't find any, so I left. A friend told me that he had a similar experience with a Nantes waiter and instead of cider the waiter had offered to bash his head in, so I got off rather lightly.

At another restaurant I had a local dish called '*civelles*' which are tiny eels cooked in wine. You see the *civelle* boats on the Loire and wonder what they are, slender craft with fine nets strung out from both gunwales. The eels are delicious but it seems a premature end for fish which have travelled three thousand miles from their birthplace in the Sargasso Sea. I tried to purchase some pâté from a *charcuterie* under the castle walls but the *patron* refused payment and presented me with a great slice saying he liked the English. To prove it he drove me to the bus station. You won't get good pâté cheaper than that.

An hour's journey by bus from Nantes brought me to the town of Guérande. The land is low and the road passes through great salt marshes which glisten in the sun. This has given rise to the theory that the Breton name — Gwen rann — meaning 'the white region' comes from the startling white of these marshes. But in Brittany there are many 'white regions' meaning the place was sacred to the Druids.

At Guerande the Druids fought hard against the monks and there is the legend of one of the more famous saints fighting a battle of magic against no less a personage than Merlin, or Marzin as he is also called locally, Arthur's sorcerer knight. Marshes were something special for Druids but apart from the cult of Ana or Anu, the earth mother, the significance is not obvious. The locality is thick with stories of triumphs over the Devil, an aphorism for Druidism.

One has a local peasant named Youenn Kerbic envious of a windmill of his own. He makes a pact with the Devil, a mill in exchange for his soul. The Lord of Wickedness had just laid the last stone when Youenn stepped forward and placed a statue of the Virgin on the top. The Devil screamed in terror and vanished. The Devil's Mill, a fine granite tower, still stands today. The Virgin is in a niche in the wall facing the sea.

Not far out of the town is a real Druid artefact, a large granite slab with the upper face chiselled perfectly flat. In the centre is cut a circular bowl. This is called the 'Fountain of the Devil' and no doubt was used by the Druids for some sacrificial rite. It was full of water and the locals say they've never seen it dry. To touch the green liquid is certain death.

There was a frog living in the bowl that seemed quite healthy and unperturbed by his deadly surroundings. I asked an old man cutting turf about this and he gave me the kind of reply with which I had scared the Parisian at the 'house of the little people' at Commana. After glancing about him fearfully he told me that the frog was no frog at all but a man who had laughed about the evil powers of the water and had drunk some.

'Don't stay here,' he told me anxiously and hurried away. I gave the frog a morsel of pâté to make him feel loved. Then I left forthwith for the City of the Legion.

I had no right to go straight to Vannes, my City of the Legion. By Nennius's sequence I should have first gone north from Bassas to Celidon, west to Castle Guinnion, then retraced my steps to Vannes then shot back up north again to Tribruit.

There is a very old story about a traveller demanding of a local how to get to such and such a place only to be told that the proposed journey was impossible from where they were and that he should start from somewhere else. Similarly there was no way of getting direct to Celidon so I would have to start from Vannes. I considered that a little cheating would do no harm.

Nennius's identification of Arthur's ninth battle as being at the City of the Legion is not so vague as it might seem. Romantic novelists have Roman legions dashing hither and thither but in modern terms this would be like moving Montgomery's Eighth Army from North Africa to Venice to quell a rising of gondoliers. No more than six legions were required to keep down the entire shaggy population of Gaul and only half this number was necessary for Britain.

The normal strength of a Roman legion was about 6,000. Each had a large and complicated administrative and supply organization, and teams of siege, road and bridge building specialists. The Romans did not achieve their conquests by indiscriminate slaughter of the native population, or by building castles for barons with private armies, but by a system of military roads, placing along them small forts garrisoned by regular troops who shuttled up and down the tracks to quell local risings.

The tactical fighting unit of the Roman army was the cohort, no more than six hundred men. The legion stayed put at its headquarters and seldom moved except for major campaigns. Thus there were only three 'Cities of the Legion' in the whole of Britain. These were Caerleon, York and Chester. But Nennius had written of *the* 'City of the Legion' and this suggests that there was no alternative to the one he had in mind. There was only one legion headquarters in the whole of Armorica and this was at Vannes, or Venetus as the Romans referred to it, the capital city of the Venetii.

Whenever Caesar mentioned the Venetii his normally peevish tone reserved for tribes unwilling to accept the blessings of Roman civilisation rose to a higher pitch of frustration and anger. Julius, never a humorous man, reported that the Gauls burst into laughter when they first saw the diminutive Roman troops.The Celts called them 'dwarves'. So he was not inclined to be lenient. But of all the Gauls, a nasty treacherous lot at best, wrote the future emperor, the Venetii are by far the worst. They had even kidnapped Roman envoys that all nations respected as inviolable. These 'envoys' had gone to requisition winter rations and there was a shortage which was starving the Celts as well. One of the worst aspects of this revolt from the Roman viewpoint was that by their bad example the Venetii encouraged other tribes to see what they could get away with. Presently they had not only been joined by neighbouring tribes, but had summoned reinforcements from Celtic Britain, an old trading partner.

Caesar would have dearly loved to have done away with the lot of them but just when he had his javelins poised for the death blow they melted away. The Venetii were in the main a seafaring people who inhabited the Atlantic coast from the Point du Raz down to the river Vilaine. After the Romans came they lived in strongholds on headlands and spits of land and the invaders could not get at them. The deep-hulled Roman galleys could approach only at high water and even then they frequently ran aground. Even the sea keeps running away, moaned puzzled Caesar. He was used to the tideless Mediterranean where it didn't.

The shallow craft of the Venetii were ideally suited to the tidal fluctuations. They were built of oak to withstand the violent seas of the Atlantic and if they did run aground they suffered little damage. And these native mariners knew the tides, rocks and currents. The Romans decided to make the Atlantic more like their home waters. They built dams to retain the sea round the enemy-held headlands so that there would always be high water. The mind boggles at the amount of work involved in this project.

But just when capitulation seemed inevitable in came the Celtic vessels, magically it seemed passing through unknown channels to take off the defenders to other strongholds and the whole process had to be repeated over again, and then again. And the Venetii knew, wrote Caesar, that we were short of grain and we would have to leave

before winter set in. But the Romans were the most deadly kind of
enemy — a persistent one. After capturing several strongholds with
nothing to show for it this brilliant general changed his tactics. He
decided to turn a sea battle which he undoubtedly would have lost to
something like a land battle at which the Romans excelled.

Gathering all his galleys together, including those reconstructed
on the banks of the Loire, Caesar put out to meet the enemy which he
put at two hundred and twenty sail. The Celts must have been confident of victory. The hulls of their vessels were too sturdy for the rams
of the frail Mediterranean galleys and their bulwarks were so high
that they gave almost complete protection from catapulted missiles.
On the other hand their missiles could be rained down on the low
open decks of the Roman vessels.

As far as the Celts could deduce the Romans had but one advantage. The galleys were propelled by oars and could manoeuvre
swiftly in any direction without regard to wind on which the cumbersome leather-sailed vessels must rely. And they did not yet know
about Caesar's secret weapon — no more than siege grappling hooks
specially mounted on long poles.

Between ten in the morning and sunset the Celts were annihilated.
Despite showers of stones the galleys paddled after the Celts and
hooked the grapnels into the rigging, then by rowing hard astern,
brought down the yards and sails. After this it was a soldier's battle
at which the Romans proved vastly superior. Caesar's boarding part-
ies swarmed aboard and made short work of the crews. The survivors tried to sail away but as luck would have it the wind fell light and
they were overtaken and suffered like the rest.

This victory ended the campaign against the Venetii. Once their
fleet had been destroyed the Celts had no means of defending their
strongholds and no escape when attacked. So they surrendered to
Roman clemency but Caesar had waited long for this moment and
he showed none. To paraphrase his words he resolved to make an
example of them to teach the rest of the natives to be more respectful
in future to Roman envoys. He executed all the leaders and sold the
rest of the population into slavery.

And so in 56 B.C. the Venetii, the Gwendawti, perished, or as British historians would have us believe, three hundred years before they
arrived from Wales to found Gwened as their capital city. The local
guide book ties itself in knots trying to explain this paradox. The
author says that the language of Gaul was very much like that of Bri-

tain and maybe only some of the Gwendawti came from Wales and the others were the survivors of the original Gaulish race. So disposing of one difficulty by creating several others the guide says with an air of desperation that anyway the Venetii were a very ancient race so we couldn't tell what actually happened.

There is a memory of an Arthurian victory over the Saxons at or near Nantes. Saint Patern or Padern, said to be a monk of the nearby monastery of Saint Gildas, was a close companion of the local chieftain named Warok throughout his many battles with the Saxons. Their last battle was in about A.D. 465 where Padern was killed, being mourned, says the hagiographer, throughout entire Brittany. This date is early for Arthur who may have been commander-in-chief but any of these dates are very approximate, an error of up to a hundred years either way being quite possible. Ambrosius Aurelianus was supposed to have begun his victorious campaign against the invaders in A.D. 470 and Gildas mentions him almost within the same breath as Badon Hill, the Celts' last victory some thirty years later.

It is perhaps no coincidence that a life of Saint Padern written in the twelfth century speaks of an encounter between the saint and Arthur. The warrior is scarcely the popular hero that the romances would have us believe. The monk author speaks contemptuously of Arthur suggesting that far from being a defender of the faith he was a hard-bargaining mercenary out for all he could get.

The 'tyrannus' Arthur bursts into Padern's cell to demand the tunic given to the saint by the Patriarch of Jerusalem. The saint refuses to hand it over, and Arthur threatens to slay him but a miracle causes the floor to open up and buries him to his chin. He has to behave before he is released from his personal dungeon.

None of the monks seemed overstruck with Arthur. Caradoc's *Life of Saint Gildas* declared that the saint's brother, called Hueil, fought against Arthur until he was captured and executed. Gildas is the family spokesman who goes to Arthur to demand compensation and the warrior pays up. Later in the same tale Arthur's wife was kidnapped by Melwas, king of Somerset, and taken to Glastonbury. Arthur turns up with an army from Devon and Cornwall and the battle is about to commence when Gildas the peacemaker arrives to negotiate 'Guennuvar's' freedom.

Arthur's wife seemed highly prone to kidnap and maybe the origin of the Round Table was not so much concerned with knightly equality but so that Arthur could examine all their faces in the hope of discovering by an unguarded glance which knight was going to take her off next.

Today the Venetii are a quiet, pleasant people living in peace in their pretty city. The moat of the tiny château is used to water the flower beds. There are window boxes on the sills and the clothes lines from the garret windows suggest that some of the defenders at least are young and feminine. Maybe this is why it is called the Château Gaillard or 'the saucy castle'.

From Vannes to the wood of Celidon is only seventy kilometres as the crow flies but the crows do not take passengers and the local buses seem as co-operative. The clerk at the bus depot consulted his timetables at length, blowing great clouds of smoke from his *Gauloises*. Then he gave up in disgust, flapping his arms and demanding to know what possessed me to want to go to Celidon. He didn't seem the kind I should tell about Arthur and he went off to get assistance and was probably struck dead for he never came back and the other clerks refused to be drawn on the subject of his whereabouts.

But I did manage to persuade them to tell me where to get a bus for Pontivy, about three-quarters of the way to Celidon, and I reached Saint Aignan at the edge of the forest just before nightfall after a walk of seventeen kilometres along the banks of the Blavet. At the café I drank nine bottles of beer to ease the desiccation of the walk in the burning sun thus causing cries of wonder and, incidentally, convincing the local drinkers that the British always drink beer in great quantities.

This suited me because I once discredited Britain on a similar score. One of the crews brought a pint beer glass into our Audierne bistro. They said that the pub owner at Falmouth had charged them thirty francs for the glass which sounded like profiteering to me, but no matter they cried, the idea was for me to demonstrate that the *Yann-Saoz* drinks glasses like that straight off and in a few seconds. There was money at stake for nobody who had not seen the feat would not believe it.

The beer of Alsace is quite unlike British beer. It is very gassy and very cold. Two gulps and I was finished, the pint was not but I was. I said that I had lost the knack. There were cries of disappointment from the believers and triumph from the doubters. The losers went off muttering that 'GB' on British cars must stand for 'Grandes Bouches' or 'Big Mouths'. In return I volunteered an opinion as to what 'F' stood for which did not improve my position. So at Saint

Aignan I retrieved the honour of the nation.

'The wood of Celyddon' is famous in Welsh legend but there is no clue to where it might have been. Geoffrey of Monmouth, although a Welshman, did not think Wales was a likely location and pushes it off to somewhere in the Midlands. Some authorities think it must be the ancient Silva Calidoniae, once the great central forest of Scotland but now vanished. A quite unfounded argument is that 'celyddon' was just a general name for every forest in Britain and could have been anywhere.

My Celidon is now called the forest of Quenecan, eighty square kilometres of woodland in central Brittany, within the rough triangle formed by Gouarec, Mur-de-Bretagne, and Silfiac. In the north-eastern corner of the forest is the artificial lake of a hydro-electric scheme which the planners have called 'Guerledon' — a Frenchified version of the ancient name. The locals know the area as 'Gerlidon' which is within monk copying error of 'Celidon' and an amazing example of survival after such a vast passage of time. Lurking amongst the leafy branches at Celidon we have three spectres, two with whom we already have passing acquaintance, the other as inevitable to our story as a wasp at a picnic.

One of the personalities in the first category is bloody Conomor, chief of Leon and Poher, sometime king of the northern Brittany province of Domnonia, the personification of evil and stock character for any monk wanting to populate a story involving dirty tricks. He appeared on the grave marker in Britain's Cornwall as father of Tristram.

British authorities are sure that Conomor was a real person of the sixth century, but they can't quite place him other than he seems to have been king of the Royal House of Domnonia which once existed in Britain, the name surviving in 'Devon', which with Cornwall roughly comprised the province. Others are not so sure. There are no British legends of Conomor and they certainly exist in Brittany, so maybe his power may have extended to the Gaulish side of the Channel. We should rather admit that Conomor must have been a Breton and that there is no real evidence that he had anything to do with Britain.

Conomor's main court was at Carhaix-Plouguer, some forty kilometres to the north-west, but in the heart of Celidon wood once stood one of his 'castles', probably no more than an earth rampart with a few huts. One legend runs that a soothsayer, not a very helpful one considering the chief's nasty disposition, told him that his fate was to die by the hand of his son. So Conomor hit on the idea of pre-natal contraception. He killed his wives, and he had several in succession, as soon as they quickened with child. He had similarly disposed of three elder brothers to come to the throne so murder was just a kind of disinfectant to Conomor.

He now proposed marriage to the daughter of Warok, chief of the Venetii whom we mentioned as a possible subordinate to Arthur, certain friend of Saint Padern, and Gildas's benefactor. Warok was not overjoyed and he agreed only after Conomor had taken a sacred oath not to kill her, which seems a reasonable request from a prospective father-in-law. The lovely Trephine lived longer than her predecessors for she actually gave birth to a baby boy. Conomor was hunting but maybe as soon as he heard of the birth the chase took place, his henchmen overtook Trephine on the Nantes road and decapitated her, leaving the baby to die in the snow.

The distraught Warok, alerted by an angel, cried out for retribution. It had been a sacred oath so the Church responded, the instrument was none other than our dear old companion of the feverish countenance, Saint Gildas. He raised Trephine from the dead and together they marched to Celidon, she carrying her severed head under her arm. Following them came the baby, also restored to life, and although no more than a week old walking on his own.

Reaching the castle Gildas threw a clod of earth at the battlements. The horrified and black-bearded faces of Conomor and his fellow murderers appeared at the window.

'Regard the justice of the Trinity,' cried Saint Gildas. At this the bastions crumbled and Conomor perished in the rubble with his accomplices. Another version of the legend has the son at the head of an army raised at Paris which defeats Conomor in battle where he is slain to fulfil the prophecy. The son then becomes a monk under Saint Gildas. Both he and his mother are reckoned to be saints in Brittany but Rome doesn't seem to know either. But this victorious son is not called Tristram as suggested by the Menabilly stone but Tremeur, in yet another version, Judval.

Three kilometres north of Saint Aignan is a small chapel dedicated to Trephine, built on the site where she was slain, or temporarily slain for after the call at the castle Gildas replaced her head on her shoulders and she lived happily ever afterwards.

The putative existence in the Dark Ages of two provinces called within a letter or so Domnonia, one in south-west Britain and the other in northern Brittany, is confusing. The reason given is the usual one that the emigrants took the name with them to Brittany as they did their possessions sometime between the third and sixth centuries, a hypothesis which seldom pauses to think that it might have happened the other way as in 'Britain' and 'Brittany'.

Irish legend records in the manner of a fairy tale how at the dawn of time Ireland was populated by three successive waves of immigrants, each doing battle with the existing occupants and driving them out. The three waves were called the Fir Bolg, Fir Gaileoin, and the Fir Domnann, not too difficult to recognize as Belgae, Gaels or Gauls, and our Dumnonii. So in fact we once had not two but three Dumnonias. But do not despair.

The generally accepted theory about the population of Western Europe is that a succession of peoples moved westwards from some point of origin in Asia Minor, the traditional Garden of Eden. These migrations were like ripples in a pool, each successive ripple of humanity, being more sophisticated (or bloody) driving the previous incumbents on westward. In their turn the new arrivals were driven on by the next wave.

If the Belgae, Gaels or Gauls, and Dumnonii arrived in Ireland in that order, and there is no reason to believe that they didn't, and they reached Britain in this order as British archaeologists say they did, why should Brittany have been the exception to this sequence of migration. The Dumnonii couldn't fly and they must have crossed the Channel from Brittany to Britain before moving across to Ireland. If the Latin writers and the Irish bards are correct this migration took place before Jesus Christ while the Saxons were still killing each other in their own country.

At one time there seems to have been no doubt where Dumnonia was. A Life of Saint Tudwal, also Tutival, Tugdual, possibly Tugen, has him born in Britain but crossing with his sister and some monks to Brittany where, says the account, his cousin Deroc was king of Dumnonia. Maybe 'Devon' is an echo of Dumnonia but it was an echo from Brittany.

We British have never been modest about theories which give us precedence, like the surprising and unlikely reverse migration from Britain to Brittany. Having sprawled the Empire over much of the earth it was a simple mental gymnastic for these Olympians to believe that before they arrived anywhere all was desert, that Britain was indeed the epicentre of humanity.

Doctor Livingstone's discovery of Lake Nyasa excited the Victorians so much they overlooked the fact that the Portuguese had discovered it many years before. Livingstone said so himself. Nor did the Empire care that it was not they who were first in Australia but the French, and that the Dutch beat them to South Africa. Native populations who must have arrived there sometime, are always ignored in stories of Great Explorations.

Our great nation should stick to discoveries that we really made. There are so many that it would be boring to list them — anyway they are so well known. But in a bar at Quimper I heard of a new British discovery whhiiich so dumbfounded me that I almost dropped my glass. A visiting British packaging consultant told me miserably that he was having great difficulty designing a box to contain five eggs.

'Five eggs?' I repeated in surprise.

'*Cinq oeufs?*' repeated the barman, making that hooting noise of incredulity that only the French can make, despite the fact he shouldn't have been listening.

'Yes, five eggs. Common Market and all that,' said my informant wearily. 'Why you damned "frogs" have to sell eggs in tens is beyond me.'

As I say this British discovery is so new that even the French have not heard that they sell eggs in tens.

7 Tintagel

I was feeling rather Conomorish when I left Saint Aignan. I was about to commit robbery without violence, but one so outrageous that it probably would go down as the crime of the century, if not of all time. Not for me mundane gold, banknotes or watches, for I was going to steal Tintagel from Britain's Cornwall and by doing so confound all those vendors of King Arthur candy and Sir Galahad ice creams and such from Camborne to Truro and Bodmin to Padstow.

The ruin on the rocky headland thrusting out into the Bristol Channel is so hallowed by tourists as the birthplace of King Arthur my intention might seem like heresy. But apart from its setting of rugged cliffs and breaking surf in the heart of supposedly King Arthur country there is no more reason why this site should have been chosen than Windsor Castle or the Waldorf Astoria. For what has been proved to be a Celtic monastery, not a castle, was never called 'Tintagel' during Arthur's time and not labelled as such until quite recently.

Geoffrey of Monmouth was the first to use the name Tintagel in his *History of the Kings of Britain*, presumably garnering this piece of information from his native sources, and he only guesses that its location was in Britain's Cornwall. Uther Pendragon's seduction of Queen Igerne by magically impersonating her husband certainly sounds like typical rollicking Celtic stuff.

The Norman compilers of the Domesday Book knew of no Tintagel. For them it was merely the monastery of the monks of Saint Petrock of Bodmin. The only castle in the area was a Norman motte and bailey. The first real castle in the manor of Bossinney, the name for 'Tintagel' in the Middle Ages, was built in A.D. 1141, one of a rash of castles which sprang up during Stephen's turbulent reign. It certainly was not called Tintagel for if it had been it would have survived for it was Henry II, the Arthurian dreamer, who had it knocked down. So the association must be false.

I found Brittany's Tintagel while searching my map for the battle-fields. On modern maps it is called Tinténiac, on earlier maps Tinté-niag and it doesn't take much imagination to interpolate this back to 'Tintagel' if it was ever called that for derivation is obscure and as far as I can discover means nothing in any of the Celtic languages.

I completed the seventy-two kilometre hike to Tinténiac in two days without much difficulty for off the main highway it is a soft, leafy walk without any major rises and falls in the land. The names of villages and hamlets, hardly more than a few cottages in most cases, are reminders of immigrant hermits, lost in the passage of time.

I passed through Saints Gwenn, Thalo, Lubin, Vran, Meen, Thual, Jauoin, and Pem. These men slew dragons, giants, dwarfs, and demons, threw blessed pebbles into the sea to drive away Saxons and pirates, cured corns, chilblains, toothache, dandruff, fits, lep-rosy, rabies, pestilence, coughs and colds, rheumatics, madness, warts, and obscure complaints now unknown to medical science.

There are more Breton saints than the whole of the rest of Christen-dom put together. Brittany has seven official founder saints, later bishops, who arrived, it is said, at the head of clans of immigrants from Britain. These are Samson, Brieuc, Malo, then called MacLou, Padern, Tugdual, and Pol-Aurelien. Just when you've memorized these you find out that certain localities have popped their own in at the expense of the approved ones.

Around Le Vieux-Marché the magnificent seven are Georges, Thiac, Lanrest, Armel the Price Bear, Farnin, Cado and a lady, Urielle. At Josselin they have Berthin, Meleuc, Mandé, Gobrien, Ser-vais, Gildas, and Cado. Trédaniel prefers Mamert, Yvertin, Lubin, Méen, Houarniaule, and another woman, Ujane. These are just a few examples and the variations can be found throughout the whole of Brittany, the only common virtue seems to have been that there was always seven — seven healers, seven monk warriors, even seven brothers and sisters. Seven was a magic or mystical number for the Celts. Three was another.

Three saints, Gwenole, Jacut, and Gweneg, are said to have been triplets. The mother, Saint Gwenn was given three breasts by God to suckle them. Evidently the monks responsible for this story were not strong on mothercraft or maybe this was just to distract attention from the fact that Gwenn was a nun and presumably a virgin.

The theme of three is repeated in the Welsh *triads* and even the trefoil rock carvings at sites as widespread as Malta, Wales, Brittany, the Orkneys, Ireland and Greece. This complex and mysterious three leafed pattern (try drawing one from memory) in a stylized form is the emblem of Breton nationalism. But due to the high mobility of the *gendarmerie nationale* these '*triskels*' have to be executed with the canned paint spray instead of a chisel.

The tombs of the seven approved founder saints used to form the route of circular pilgrimage about Brittany called '*Tro-Briezh*'. The 525 kilometre penitential journey, passing through Dol, Saint Malo, Treguir, Saint Pol de Leon, Quimper, and Vannes, was accomplished in easy daily stages of roughly twenty kilometres with frequent stops at roadside shrines and holy wells. The favoured times of the year — Easter, Pentecost, Saint Michel (28 September), and Christmas.

During and after the Black Death, said to have been the main instigator of the pilgrimages, as many as three thousand pilgrims are recorded as visiting the tomb of Saint Padern at Quimper on each occasion. The granite Christian obelisks you see on the roadside in Brittany called '*calvaires*' — the carvings depict the life of Jesus Christ — are also said to have been the manifestation of the despair of the population at the terrible pestilence. Brittany was inflicted to such a degree that on seeing the good struck down as well as the evil people began to turn back to the old Druid religion. The Church countered this with Saint Anne, the original earth mother cult, which satisfied both needs. The Revolution put an end to the *Tro-Briehz* altogether.

Possibly the oddest saint in Brittany is Saint Diboan who is celebrated in the Quimper district. '*Diboan*' in Breton means 'without pain'. He is not one but two saints so with prayer to him you double your chances of a cure. He is known in our village as '*tu-pe-tu*'. It is an expression we used on the boats when mackerel fishing meaning you have had above average luck, catching fish on both sides of the boat or wherever you care to drop your line in the water. It is also used sarcastically. '*Tu-pe-tu, gaarst*', an angry fisherman will tell you with an expression like a boot full of water. At the same time he flicks the underside of his chin with the back of his hand. This means he has caught nothing. '*Gust*' or '*Gaarst*' is a useful word in Breton. It can be used as a short sharp expletive sounding like a squib or drawn out to express surprise or outrage. I had been using it for years in conversations with old ladies until it was kindly pointed out to me that it meant 'whore'.

Despite my expectation Tinténiac was an Arthurian disappointment. Arthur or Arzur was certainly known in the village but I could not even find the remains of a Celtic monastery let alone a castle which would have served as a birthplace of the great warrior, only a canal with small yachts with owners dressed for big yachts. The surrounding country was unpopulated, flat and wild marshland cut about with small channels or ditches, '*frutes*' as they are called locally. I found nothing that would have induced Arthur to have been born there although according to legend he didn't have much time to cast about, being given birth immediately after the bedsport. Uther Pendragon seems to have had to jump clear and only a Celtic legend would not have us suspecting a prior conception.

I got into conversation with the local curé who was reckoned to be an authority on Celtic legend but he had not heard of any association of Arthur's birth with Tinténiac. But he said that Artor the Bear God was supposed to have originated locally. The cult was very strong even well into the Middle Ages.

He invited me in for a chat but at first seemed more interested in the mosquito bites on my forehead. I was sorry about this preoccupation for his lotion contained some bright red dye which despite daily scrubbing still looked like an outbreak of a highly contagious disease over a week later.

The curé was a cautious little man with grey hair cropped within a quarter of an inch. One could easily imagine him in the isolation of his mahogany confessional, deliberating problems and penances. Before replying to my questions he drew his face into a contemplative grimace, screwing his eyes into tight balls under the spectacles with the broken frame mended with adhesive tape.

He offered me a glass of wine but before drinking it he waved the sign of the cross over it in the unconcerned way you shake out a match. He gave the same blessing to the sweet cake which he produced from his vestry cupboard and cut with a penknife produced from the pocket of his worn and faded cassock.

He said he knew of a legend of Arthur stopping a giant named Dinabuc stealing the daughter of a king of Armorica from Mont Saint Michel. I knew the story for Wace had written about it in his *Roman de Brut*. I wondered what the king was doing at the island cathedral for it is across the border in Normandy, a theft for which the Bretons blame the River Couesnon:

Le Couesnon,
Par sa folie
A mit le mont,
En Normandie

'When the Bretons arrived here there was no frontier, remember,'
he replied. The Normans had not swept south into the land of the
Franks until the seventh century at the earliest. I asked him about a
problem that had been puzzling me for some time, did he think it possible that a conquered people could invade a land full of Gauls? He
said he couldn't answer that one. He was being tactful so I put the
question another way. Did he think that the land had no native population, a wasteland created by the Romans.

The curé said that he didn't think that was possible then he smiled.
He said he was wondering whether I was trying to get him to deny the
teaching of his Church. He would not do that but he would tell me
something that might put me on the right track.

When the Romans came Brittany was part of Gaul, he told me. In
this region the Gaulish tribe was the Curiosilites. To the east of here
were the Dioblintes, and to the west the Osismii. To the south-west
were the Venetii, and to the south of them the Namnetes. It was a
strange fact, said the curé, that the dialects spoken in Brittany today
conform remarkably to the ancient territories of these tribes. And
with subtle local variations the Breton costumes also conformed to
these tribal divisions. This was exciting. I pressed him further. If that
is so, I said, what we see in Brittany today are not the descendants of
emigrants from Britain at all, but the remnants of the Gauls. It is the
French that are the invaders, not the Bretons.

The curé smiled, 'Did I say that? Dear me. You *will* have me deny-
ing the teachings of my Church. Let's change the subject. What do
you do at Dol? Will you find your Arthur there?'

I replied that I couldn't be sure but I hoped to find one of his companions, for I suspected that Dol had been visited by Tristram and
Iseult. The earliest surviving account of the episode is the twelfth-century poem by the Norman Beroul. According to the poet King
Mark's court is at a place called Lancien which was near the monastery of Saint Samson.

Tristram and Iseult and a number of companions arrive at Lancien after a long journey and go up to the great monastery by a paved
road. The great baron Dinas the Brave has brought with him as a

present a garment of rich silk of immense value. Nobody had even seen anything so wonderful. Iseult lays the garment on the high altar as an offering and it is later made into a chasuble and used only once a year at the feast of Saint Samson. According to Beroul the chasuble was still kept at the monastery.

The greatest romance in the Arthurian cycle has been linked by British historians with Lantyne in Britain's Cornwall. There was a resemblance between the name and Beroul's Lannion. Also there was a parish church under the patronage of Saint Sampson (he has a 'p' as in England). This church is the vestige of a monastery said to have been founded by the saint. And of course Mark is thought to have been king of Britain's Cornwall. Nearby was the earthwork called Castle Dor which might have been his court. This makes a lot of sense.

But for the Bretons Mark, Tristram and Iseult were Bretons and so was Saint Samson after he came to Brittany. And the great monastery of Saint Samson is at Dol, not a parish church but a great ecclesiastical foundation established by the saint when he arrived in A.D. 550. Breton tradition says that he was given the land by a local magnate in gratitude for curing his wife of leprosy and driving the crabs out of the head of his mad daughter.

The curé was quite surprised that Samson had been transferred to an obscure monastery in south west England. Not only was Samson one of the seven founder saints he was the chief evangelizer of Brittany. But the hagiographers do have Samson originating in Britain. He is said to have been a former Archbishop of York, then the premier see in Britain, although the curé doubted he would have given up his senior appointment to come to Brittany as a simple monk of his own free will. Maybe my theory of the longhairs being replaced by the tonsures had something to do with his departure to Brittany but it is doubtful whether he would have relinquished such a powerful position so easily. What was even more unlikely was that a great archbishop would have established a monastery in far away and wild Cornwall.

But the curé thought my identification of Lancien with the famous Lannion was too ambitious. The distance from Lannion to Dol was almost one hundred kilometres and Beroul says that the court was near Dol. Neither had he heard of a historic chasuble there. There was one at Loannec, a few kilometres from Lannion, but this is thought to have belonged to Saint Yves who lived there in the thirteenth century.

Of Dinas the bold and brave baron there certainly were echoes near Dol — the ancient cities of Dinan and Dinard. Perhaps the giver of the rich garment was a city in allegorical form or perhaps Dinas had given his name to them. Maybe he might have even been Arthur for Dinard comes from '*din arz*' meaning 'the hill of the bear'. Dinan just means 'fortress'.

'Have you yet been to Pleumeur-Badou near Lannion?' the curé asked suddenly. I shook my head, but asked him what prompted the question.

'Oh nothing,' he replied, 'except that Arthur is supposed to have been buried there after he was killed at Camlann. ' He was enjoying the impact that this casual statement had on me.

'Why do they say that?' I asked.

'No more than an association of names. Just off the coast there is an Isle of Avel. Could be Avalon,' he said.

'Do you think so?' I asked him.

'No. The island is solid granite. You would need explosives to bury Arthur there,' he replied.

We had another glass of wine then I said I must go. With simple country courtesy he said he would see me on my road and walked a considerable distance with me talking as we went.

He said it was quite refreshing to meet an obvious pagan. He suspected some of his parishioners of paganism but they regularly attended Mass and knew their catechism so they passed for good catholics. But, said the curé, he sometimes gained the impression when he discussed God that he was trying to sell a new newspaper.

As though he had seen an invisible line of the road the old curé stopped and offered me his hand.

'Mont Dol is an evil place. May God be with you,' he said. I thanked the kind man and continued on my way. He was still standing at the same spot when I turned a bend in the road and he passed from view.

Like the curé had said I had found that most of my acquaintances in Brittany were indifferent to if not contemptuous of Christianity. Perhaps this coolness is a hangover from the militant anti-clericalism of the Revolution which after all was less than two hundred years ago. The general attitude seems to be that the majority of priests are so divorced from reality that they can't be taken seriously.

The priests that do make an impression in a fishing community succeed because they behave like ordinary mortals and have some understanding of what the fishermen go through. A curé who surprises a crew at a café at eight o'clock in the morning and looks down his nose without a thought that these same men have just come ashore after perhaps fifteen days on a stinking fishing boat, being soaked and bruised mentally and physically, will stand little chance of success in a village like Lervily.

Apart from seeing him in the pulpit I did not know the curé at Esquibien, the seat responsible for the spiritual affairs of the commune of which Lervily is a part. But I have met the rector on several occasions, a small, quiet man in a shabby suit and an old woollen scarf. It was the rector who cycled to Lervily to perform the last rites for the dying and the offices for the dead.

All the villagers know him and give him a cheery wave for he is a kind man and his words of comfort for the bereaved make some kind of sense and he talks to them in Breton, not a language which has found much favour with the Church. I shall never forget the first time I met the rector.

With the rest of the crew of my crabber we were at Tante'phine's splitting a litre of wine. A litre of wine divides almost exactly into six glasses and this is why a Breton fishing boat always carries six men. They say so anyway. The glasses had been poured but not yet touched. We lit our cigarettes and rested back in our chairs savouring the peace, comfort and dryness of it all.

'Here comes the rector,' cried the skipper and the glasses were swigged off in one gulp before I got a hand to mine. But I didn't care very much. I wasn't going to be hustled along by any churchman and took a slow sip at my glass and returned it nearly full to the table. Théophile appeared to be seized by panic and swept my glass to his lips and finished in a gulp. I let out a cry of protest which was cut short by the entry of the rector into the bistro. He shook hands with each of us and then went off for a few words with old Tante'phine. I thought he could not have been fooled for a moment for the empty bottle and the six glasses were still on the table. And it was unlikely that a crew would have been in a bistro without having a drink. I was inclined to be snappy. The rector finished his business and, bidding us a good day, departed. Tante'phine put another litre of wine on the table without a word.

'You don't understand,' said the skipper. 'The rector always buys us a litre if he sees we have nothing to drink.'

The curé had told me that the best way to approach Mount Dol was from the west. It was a circuitous route but at Châteauneuf I would easily find lodgings for the night. This is how I missed the road and stumbled across the hamlet of Saint Guinoux and a strange tale which ran contrary to the usual Christian theme of the triumph of good over evil. I can only attribute this to the power of Druid's rock which I knew lay not far away across the marshland to the east.

Just to the south-west of Saint Guinoux, I was told, there once was a village called Coquenaille which stood in a forest clearing. Satan sought to enrage the Christians with a plague of crows. He brought nests from the rest of Gaul and the cawing was so incessant that it stopped the masses and drove the villagers mad. The good curé prayed to God for help and was no doubt gratified when an angel dressed in black appeared to ask him what was up.

'Up?' cried the monk, for it was a long time ago. Could the angel be deaf? 'For God's sake do something about those crows. Anything . . .'

'I don't know about "for God's sake",' said Satan, for the dark angel was he. 'But do you really mean "anything"?'

'Yes, anything,' cried the holy man, his voice rising to a scream in his frustration.

Satan had. The sea roared over the coast and drowned the crows and a considerable part of north-eastern Brittany as well. For the year was A.D. 709 when an '*immensi tremor oceani*' tilted the land, created the Channel Islands and Mont Saint Michel out of high ground, drowned a large number of coastal towns and villages with their populations, and made marshland out of what was forest and lush pasture.

There can be little doubt that the earthquake of the legend is historical fact. The Romans spoke of the vast forest which they called Sessicum which once stretched from Mont Saint Michel, then called Tumba Belini, the tomb of the Gaulish sun god Belenus, to Dinard, later the home of gods called the 'milords', the English aristocrats who changed the city into a little England about the turn of this century.

The names of some of the drowned towns and villages are known to us — Porspican, Thomen, La Feu, Hestre, Maury, Saint Anne, Saint Louis, and Saint Etienne. And probably the inundation was the end of the great Ker Is, the fabulously rich capital of King Gradlon of Brittany's Cornwall.

Life in the city must have been precarious. The legend says that only the massive city walls prevented flooding at high water, and the ramparts were fitted with sluices — the reason for these is obscure other than to help the legend along — which were kept locked. Only King Gradlon had the keys and he kept them on a gold chain round his neck. His daughter, a rich, beautiful nymphomaniac who like the Australian dream woman probably owned a pub as well, was the deer in the legend of King Marc'h of Cornwall — Dahud, Ahés, or Morgane.

One stormy night as she lay in bed thinking about whatever rich beautiful nymphomaniacs think about, she heard a voice calling her from outside the city walls. Looking out of the window she saw a handsome youth, the only flaw in his character being that he was Satan in disguise and bent on the destruction of Gradlon for the king was strong in the church. Dahud sneaked into the sleeping king's bedroom and stole the keys. Climbing once again to the battlements she throws them down to Satan who races round the sluices unlocking them.

Warned by God that evil work was afoot, a monk arrived across the causeway which connected Ker Is with the mainland. He is none other than Saint Gwenolé. He awakens the king and — a nice touch this — they feed their horses on eggs to give them stamina to race the encroaching sea to the coast. The legend is short of horses for there were only two in the entire city. Gwenolé mounts one and Gradlon the other with his daughter riding behind him. But Gradlon's horse is unequal to the task and Gwenolé persuades the king to throw Dahud into the waves and she perishes. The monk and the king reach dry land safely.

On dark stormy nights you can hear the sobbing and plaintive cries of Dahud above the roaring seas, and the bells of the lost Ker Is. So strong is this legend that French archaeologists have made serious attempts to trace the city, all unsuccessful, except the find of some sculptured masonry on the coast near the port of Douarnenez in the middle of the nineteenth century. It was of this discovery that Claude Debussy wrote his descriptive piano piece *La Cathédrale engloutie*.

Saint Guinoux, now no more than a few cottages, was once a Roman stronghold and before they came there was a temple to Belenus and also to Gargant, the giant god, the latter borrowed by Rabelais for his life of the inestimable Gargantua, father of Pantagruel.

Later there was a temple to Lug who was a handy god to have around.

According to Irish legend, Lug, always called 'of the long arm' and 'the many skilled', had one of those debates with a city gatekeeper used by Celtic bards to display the accomplishments of their characters. Lug said he was a carpenter. The gatekeeper said they already had one. Lug then says in turn that he is a smith, warrior, harpist, poet, historian, hero, sorceror, and so forth. The gatekeeper said that it was a pity but they'd got one of each of those as well. So Lug sticks his spear down the guardian's throat making his earlier patience with the man seem superfluous.

I remember that village bed clearly. The night was hideous with large unidentifiable insects which flew so clumsily about the room that I wondered if they'd ever done it before. Worse were elephantine mosquitoes which bated me with stingers in all the places left undyed by the curé at Tinténiac. So venomous was this attack that I was driven out of bed and I saw the Devil's Rock silhouetted against the first flush of dawn, two-humped like a black camel.

At Dol the epic struggle between Celtic Christianity and Druidism is perpetuated in symbolic form. The legends abound of two rival factions locked in mortal combat. It is giant against dwarf, Light against Darkness, Arthur against, strangely, Normans, two armies led by rival brothers who bled each other so copiously that it turned the wheel of a water mill. God put a stop to this last battle by throwing a rock from Heaven which landed between the antagonists. The heavenly thunderbolt stands outside the city on the road to Kamborn, a great menhir in shocking pink granite. The site is called 'the field of sorrow'.

Possibly the symbolism of the future will be extended to include gendarmerie against parking motorists or competing guides, for the city appeared to be full of both. These battles were being waged relentlessly in what would turn out to be the hottest summer of the century.

Samson's monastery is now an imposing Gothic cathedral. His stone coffin was here but it vanished sometime in the mid-nineteenth century leaving a hole in the floor under circumstances described by the guide with bushy eyebrows as 'une scandale terrible'. The crowd gasped in horror and waited patiently for him to continue but he didn't. It was left to me to ask the obvious question but to my dismay the guide sat down on a chair and buried his head in his hands. The audience started shooting me angry looks as if I were responsible for the whole thing so I moved on. Evidently it was all to do with black magic rites but nobody seemed sure. My informant said the guide didn't know either and his breakdown was his usual way of getting out of a sticky corner. Not a bad idea but it might have got me lynched.

Samson was not only senior primate of Brittany but also played the part of king maker. Conomor had married the widow of Prince Iona of Domnonia. Needless to say it was old Blue Beard who had widowed her. But she already had a son named Judual who prudently fled to Paris, to the court of King Childerbert of the Franks, to avoid his logical end.

The years passed until the primate came to the conclusion that it was time for the prince to return to Domnonia to claim the throne and unseat Conomor. He went to Paris to fetch him but Queen Ultragoth would not let handsome Judual go and taking a leaf from Conomor's book she tried to murder the saint using the ritual three times. She reckoned without Divine intervention. Before drinking his poisoned wine Samson made the customary sign of the cross and the glass shattered. A mad horse that she lent him for a canter became docile, and a lion let loose in his cell dropped dead. The queen took to laughing and catcalling at his masses but the humour was cut short with 'a sudden bloody flux to the mouth' and she joined the lion.

Far from being angry Childerbert lent the two Bretons an army which marched to Brittany and met Conomor at the foot of the Montagnes d'Arrée, near a place still called quaintly Brank Aleg, 'the willow branch'. The fight raged for three days until, on the evening of the third, after a prayer to God, Conomor dropped dead. An enormous slab of slate marks the tyrant's grave at the village of Mengluez not far from Brank Aleg. It is called Menbeg Konmor. Do not be concerned, dear reader, for we have not heard the last of him yet.

The great outcrop of rock called Mont Dol rears out of the marshes ten kilometres north of the city. It is reckoned to have been the most important Druid site in the whole of Armorica and towering an awesome sixty-five metres above an otherwise flat terrain it looks the part.

I sweated up the narrow road to the summit wondering what I would find, pools of blood, perhaps the odd angel's wing or a broken harp. Instead I found this ancient site was a gigantic rubbish dump of plastic bottles, ice cream wrappers and paper bags. It was lunch time and I was alone but above the paper rustling in the wind I could hear an uncanny shrill twittering and tapping. I was glad I had Arthur, Gildas and Taliesin with me for the clamour was rising in intensity and for quite a time I could not see anything that might account for it. After much searching I found the answer in a robin which was furiously attacking another bogus robin in the shape of a label on an empty tomato juice can.

The two-humped summit is uneven and strewn with boulders. Amongst the rocks Saint Michael, the chief angel, took on Satan to decide whether Right or Wrong should prevail. The contest included swordplay and sporting activities such as running, leaping higher than the other, wrestling, and putting the rock, and singing, dancing, harp-playing, and even flying. Saint Samson acted as referee, a rash concession on the part of Satan, so there was no doubt about the outcome but there seems to have been some rules or fair play for various rocks are neatly labelled so the competitors knew their corners.

Here is 'Saint Michael's Seat' and 'Satan's Bench'. There is 'Saint Michael's Mitre Stand' and 'Satan's Rock' and 'Satan's Club'. In the centre of the arena is where Saint Michael's sword struck the rock and opened up a hole into which Satan fell. But he shot out again and flew to the north-east hump where you can see his claw marks. Saint Michael's horse left some hoof marks on the lower south-east knoll.

Having displaced the Druids who worshipped the sun the Romans built a temple on the mount dedicated to Diana the Huntress, virgin goddess of the moon, and sister of Apollo, who himself was a sun god. The Mithraic cult of the bull which broke out in the Roman army was also celebrated here. Of all this nothing remains except a souvenir of the Druids, a small spring which now bubbles into a concrete cistern, and what is described in the guide books as the remains of a stone circle which requires great imagination to see. For Christianity there is the small cell of Notre Dame d'Espérance and a stone cross.

I could hear the rubbish distributors climbing the sacred mountain and it was time to leave. Sadly and inexplicably the tomato can robin had beaten its live opponent and the small bird's lifeless and bloody body lay amongst the wastepaper. I buried him in a hole scooped in the soft turf and then descended the track. Near the bottom I met a family car trying to drive up the slope. They are a fearless race the French.

I couldn't face the heat of the saint's city so that night my small party slept among the willows at the foot of the mount. Despite the large number of stagnant pools and ditches the mosquitoes did not come with the dying sun. Maybe they went to Dol where the blood was richer.

8   Castle Guinnion and Tribruit

Off the road from Dol is a small leafy lane lined by Menhirs which lead up to a hill called Menez Garro. The British Cornish have a legend about the old capital of Cornwall — like them all a rich city of many splendours. But the women were wicked and given to drinking and worse while the men were underground mining tin. So God interrupted the dance with a flood and Langarrow was swept away. No remains of the city have ever been found and the legend could be a memory of what happened in Brittany in A.D. 709. The local Breton legend says that the hill was the site of a great city but it was flooded, a strange event for a hill. But 'garro' in Breton merely means 'deer' and this is too flimsy evidence for a positive association.

I crossed the river Rance by the highway bridge from Saint Servan to the outskirts of Dinard. Dinard is as pleasant a seaside town as you'll find anywhere and well chosen by what the guide books call '*la gentry brittanique*' for its colony. But after a meal I struck off to the south-west and arrived at Tregon in the early afternoon. So I reached the site of Arthur's eighth victory over the Saxons — the battle of Castle Guinnion.

This battlefield has been tentatively identified in Britain as Binchester in County Durham. The reason for this choice is that the Roman name for the town was 'Vinovia'. 'Vindo' is 'white' in Latin and 'Guin', the first syllable of Guinnion, is 'white' in Old Welsh. To my mind the scholars have been trying really hard with this one.

Below me was the River Guennon, the first syllable also means 'white' in Breton so I have already qualified the place by British standards. 'Guin' as in the Nennius spelling would mean 'wine' in Breton and the great river is not renouned for its 'bouquet' and hereabouts vineyards are as rare as hen's teeth. The Guennon flows into the English Channel between Pen Guen and Saint Jacut de la Mer. On the eastern bank standing high above the river, is Castel Guennon — 'the white castle' — but how it got its name is a mystery.

In A.D. 560 Chrames, the rebel son of Clotaire I of the Franks, fled to Armorica to Castel Guennon, with his wife, daughter and son. Nothing more exemplifies the power of the Franks in Armorica at this period, the Arthurian period when the homeless waifs from Britain are reputed to have conquered Brittany, than the fact that the army for the siege was raised locally from Gauls on direct orders from Paris. Where were the British then?

The siege ran on and eventually the leader of the besiegers set fire to the castle and luckless Chrames and his family were cremated alive. There are no prizes for guessing the identity of the perpetrator of this terrible deed. Oddly enough Conomor's headquarters at this time were said to have been at Lannsiec, not far from Dinard and very close to Dol. Could this be the court of King Mark referred to by Beroul as 'Lancien'? The account mentions a site alongside a river — the Rance in this case — and a cave where Samson slew a dragon when he arrived at Dol. From Lannsiec — it is called Lancieux on modern French maps — a causeway leads across the marshes to the monastery, the 'paved road' taken by Tristram, Iseult and Dinas the Brave. Arthur was not implicated in the folk memory of the seige, but a namesake does occur in the later history of Castel Guennon or Château Guildo as it came to be called.

In the fifteenth century a noble young rake named Gilles de Bretagne and his friends used the castle for a series of orgies which would have rivalled those of Sir Francis Dashwood's Hellfire Club. So infamous in fact that Guildo has passed into French vernacular in the expression '*courir le guilledon*'. The English equivalent would be 'chasing crumpet'.

It was well that Gilles enjoyed life for he shortly left it under terrible circumstances. Short of cash he intrigued against his elder brother, François I, Duke of Brittany, who is remembered under the soubriquet 'well-beloved'. Arthur de Montauban, a man with an ear at court and the duke's friend, told him that the King of France had heard about the intrigue and did not want a civil war on his borders. Unless Gilles was disposed of, the king would bring an army to Brittany and appoint another duke.

So François imprisoned his young brother at his château of La Hardouinais in central Brittany, in one of those cramped dungeons known appropriately as an '*oubliette*'. Despite these privations Gilles refused to die. The duke had him brought out and treated him to a poisoned banquet, but Gilles survived. So the 'well-beloved' had him strangled.

A strange funeral superstition survives in the locality of Castel Guennon which can only be a hangover from the Druid death ritual, the last crossing to the Isle of the Wind. The custom was practised generally in Brittany until the end of the last century. Before burial a corpse has to cross water and always from the right to the left bank, from east to west so to speak. The ferrymen who performed this service were held in superstitious awe, for each time they were making a token voyage to the Otherworld. The duty was kept within a family and handed down from generation to generation. Tremener is not an uncommon family name in Brittany and it comes from the word 'tre-menvan' meaning 'the dead one'.

I saw one of these funerals on my way out of Guildo. There is a bridge so a boat is no longer necessary for the ritual. But there is something more. Whenever the cortège passes a roadside shrine it halts and a cross of bay branches is laid momentarily at the foot of the coffin. I asked what this meant. A bearer told me that he didn't really know but it was 'to help the soul sleep'.

Some of the crosses or '*calvaires*' were so old they were hardly recognisable as such. The form of the Celtic cross, the circle of granite with a cross cut into its surface, has been the cause of much dispute as to its origin. Seeing those worn crosses with the carving weathered away so leaving only a knob like a chess set bishop prompted the thought that the form was more utilitarian than artistic. Unlike marble, granite — and Celtic countries are mostly granite — is fragile, difficult to work and the risk of knocking off one of the arms of the cross would be high. The cross within a circle held no such risk and it would last much longer. For posterity choose a Celtic cross.

On my left as I left Guildo were the ruins of one of the largest cities in Brittany, Corseul, the capital of the tribe called the Curiosolites, the allies of the Venetii. As their name implies they were an inquisitive people, fond of interfering and Julius Caesar did not love them. He kept sending cohorts to rap their knuckles, and on one occasion during the great rebellion an entire legion under Marcus Trebius Gallus. There survives an epitaph to a Roman soldier's mother, and her son's inscription makes you feel as if you knew them. It reads:

C 'Consecrated to the shades of the departed for Silicia Namgidde, who through her love left her home in Africa to follow me here where she lies. She died at the age of sixty-five years. Her son Caius Flavius Januarius raised this stone.'

The other ally of the Venetii was the Osismii, whose chief city was at Lesneven, a small town to the north-east of Brest. These were peaceful fisherfolk and Caesar sniffed at these rock-hoppers. Julius was a true soldier. Outraged when a tribe fought back at him, contemptuous when it didn't.

Having already visited the City of the Legion at Vannes I could ignore the ninth and go direct to Arthur's battle number ten, saving me at least ninety kilometres for the return journey, for Tribuit lies along the coast from Guildo, about seventy-six kilometres west then north-west. But two large towns lay in my path and to avoid them, or rather pass quickly through them, I took a bus.

Unfortunately for this idea the bus turned out to be a '*tour scénique organisé* a fact kept secret by the lady clerk who sold me the ticket, so I found myself jammed between sixty men and women. All the men seemed to be wearing garish nylon track suits and white cloth caps, and the women, great fat things with varicose veins on their legs like maps of the Routes Nationales of France, must have bought a job lot of yellow dresses with a large sunflower motif. They were excited, boisterous, and noisy and it was only a matter of time before the pestilence of community singing was upon us.

Unlike the English who at such times attempt to sing with their mouths shut, the French sing like their cavalry charges, each trying to outdo the others. And so we roared through some of the finest scenery in Europe to the strains of a French music hall song called 'Jam sticks everywhere'. The chorus leader was the largest lady with thick dark hair under her arms and a voice which could be copied with advantage by Trinity House.

I began to think bloody thoughts, how I'd like to throw them naked into beds of stinging nettles, how I wished we'd be hijacked by Conomor . . .

Fat Lady: 'You are an English, *monsieur*?'

Me: 'Yes.'

Fat Lady: 'Ol-la-la. I like well the English. Now a little English song, if you please.'

Me: 'Me?'

Fat Lady: 'Yes.'

Me: 'No.'

Fat Lady: 'Yes.'

Me (singing) '*Alou-et-ta, gentile alou-et-ta . . .*'

Fat Lady: 'One moment, *monsieur*, that is not an English but a French song.'

Me: 'Never.'

Fat Lady: 'I repeat, *monsieur*, that is a French song. (*shrewdly*) If that is an English song, pray tell what is an *alouette*?'

Me: 'The name of a young lady.'

Fat Lady: 'Liar. It is a bird that goes tweet-tweet in the sky.'

Me: 'Never.'

Fat Lady: 'I tell you, *monsieur*, it is a . . .'

But we had arrived at Lanleff. I did not have to make any effort to leave the bus for I was swept out by the tide that wanted to '*faire pipi.*' Amazingly enough the Fat Lady fell backwards into a bed of stinging nettles, legs up, drawers round her ankles. I will never again doubt the efficacy of prayer.

At Lanleff is a circular tower which is a Gaulish temple, Roman temple, Druid temple, part of a parish church since fallen down, a cathedral that never got up, and a cell built by monks from Britain. It depends which guide book you read. The concensus is for the view that it is the ruin of a Benedictine monastery dedicated to Saint Magloire which fell down in A.D. 1148. Two guide books say this so Benedictine abbey it is by a majority of one. But one of these two goes as far as to suggest that the ruin is positive evidence that the Bretons discovered America.

'There exists at Newport, Rhode Island, USA,' writes the author, obviously just back from a heavy lunch, 'a ruined tower of circular plan, not without resemblance to the temple at Lanleff, which could only have been built by the Bretons and at a similar date.' Thus he concludes, the Bretons arrived in North America before '*Erik le Rouge*' and his Norsemen, well before the galleons of Christopher Columbus. A little snag is that '*Erik le Rouge*' died one hundred and thirty years before the suspected date of the tower but the rest of it is good stuff. This kind of thinking would have brought the author to the fore in the Stone Age, or made him a thorough-going searcher for Arthurian battlefields.

At Lanleff amongst the pines, Old Man's Beard, and lavatory paper is the source river at the mouth of which Arthur fought his tenth battle — the river Tribruit. The debate over the whereabouts of

this battlefield has been somewhat complex and at times threatened
to bring Nennius down altogether for the various versions of the manuscript differ so widely. The renderings include 'Trahtreuruit', 'trach-
theuroit', 'ribbroit', and 'robroit'. Two versions do however agree on
'tribruit'. But there is no agreement on what the name means or
where the river is except that it may be in the north, possibly south-
western Scotland. So enigmatic is this river that at least one authority was for substituting 'beach' for 'river' thus widening the search to
include the entire British coastline.

The river at Lanleff is now called the Trieaux which is half and half
Breton and French for 'three waters'. If the name was rendered
entirely in Breton it would be Trifruit or Trifrouit. One may recall
the central Brittany river with the Christmassy name as an example
— the Brandi*frouit*.

The river takes its name from the right angled junction it makes
with the river Le Leff opposite the picturesque château called the
Roche-Jagu. Both rivers are clear, swift flowing and wooded. There
is the scent of pine in the air and also of the sea for we were not far
upstream from the small fishing port of Lezardrieau — 'the cove of
the three waters'. You can hear the silence and Tribruit is as nice a
place to get killed or maimed as you could wish for. But there seemed
to be no legend concerning Arthur or rather nobody I could ask
about him. I could have consulted the warrior as he stood behind me
gazing down the river but one of the rules for my mental companions
was that I could not ask them anything I did not know. That went for
Arthur, and Gildas and Taliesin as well.

No one I talked to at the fishing port had heard of an ancient battle
on the river, nor had they at Paimpol, four kilometres to the east, nor
west at Treguier on the banks of the river Jaudy, the next estuary
along the coast. I found another saint at this last place — Saint Tugdual, who it may be remembered came to Brittany in the sixth century to stay with King Deroc of Domnonia, a cousin. I wonder if the
king was pleased to see him for the ecclesiastical history says he
brought with him not only his beautiful sister, Saint Sew, but seventy-
two monks and his mother, Saint Pompée, as well. Like freckles
saints ran in the family. At Treguier he slew his entry dragon, built
his first monastery of which nothing is left, and commenced to order
the lives of the new Bretons.

From Treguier to the city of Perros Guirec is just twenty kilometres and it took me just four hours to walk. I had become very

good at walking. My feet were sound and my thighs no longer ached although I had worn out my second pair of tennis shoes. But walking now took no conscious effort. And I became amazingly accurate about predicting how long a journey on foot would take me. Unlike with motor cars where moving at thirty or fifty kilometres an hour is a matter of foot pressure and the amount of traffic on the road, everybody seems to have a natural walking speed, a combination of length and frequency of stride. The number of pedestrians on the road makes no difference to this pace.

David Livingstone could predict within a week how long a walk of thousands of miles across Africa would take him. I found that I walked at five kilometres an hour and after measuring the distance on the map did some quick division and I would be there within a few minutes of my prediction. But walking has hazards. Livingstone had fever and spears. Mine were interesting conversations at garden gates or in bistros.

Between the lighthouse and the Beg ar Sqewel at Perros are a large number of blocks of pink granite, a feature of this coast. These are said to be petrified people or animals, sorcerors, dwarves, King Arthur's Head, and dancing maidens turned to stone for cavorting on the Sabbath. A great turret of rose-coloured rock in 'The Devil's Castle.' You can stand on your hands, lie on your side, close one eye, close both if you like, look at them from any direction or angle and you won't see the faintest resemblance to what they are supposed to be.

Me to Guide: 'I can't see a pig in that.'

Guide: 'But, monsieur, can you not see its face, and ears, and snout?'

Me: 'No.'

Guide: '. . . and the little curly tail?'

Me: 'No, I can't.'

Guide: 'Monsieur, you are looking at the wrong rock.'

Me: 'Sorry. Which one then?'

Guide: 'That one there.'

Me: 'But you said that one was the wizard.'

Guide: 'Did I? Pardon, monsieur, that one over there, then.'

Not far away is the little twelfth-century chapel of Saint Kineg where there is a statue of the saint that you have to stick pins into. If you can then you will be married within twelve months. If you can't you will never marry. I could hear little screams of annoyance from little madames of the future who were having a tough time, having brought their boyfriends along to take the hint. The statue is of granite. I asked a man who was pointing a broom at some rubbish in a desultory manner the origin of this unworkable superstition.

'Oh that, gust,' he said. 'The old Saint Kineg used to be of wood. I must take that notice down sometime'.

Off the headland with the rocks are the *Seizh Enezenn* — 'the seven islands' — to which no boatman will take you no matter how much you offer him, the guide told me. It was the haunt of '*ar Gwrac'h goz*' — 'the old witch' — and the great black sea crow, the '*morvran*', the 'bird of the dead'. But his brother might be persuaded to take me. I said that his brother was a hero and deserved the *Légion d'honneur* and I wouldn't think of putting him to all the trouble. If I changed my mind, the guide told me, his brother's boat was near the lighthouse of Porz Konomor. I did not know until then that 'Old Mobile Catastrophe' had ever been in the shipping business.

The highest point in Brittany is Menez Bré which is about twenty-six kilometres from Perros. I took a bus because the road is an expressway and even with my new slippers I just couldn't manage the legal minimum speed. From the top of this small mountain you can see most of Brittany's Cornwall but I hadn't come entirely for the view. At Pedernec legend preserves the name of a Druid, almost a unique event. His name was Kian Gwenc'hlan, the second name meaning 'of the white (or holy) race'. He was blind and a bard and a prophet.

Another dweller on the mountain was a monk named Machoarvien which made Frenchmen ill so they changed his name to Hervé. Hervé was born in A.D. 515 in Leon, a monk who wasn't born in Britain is also an almost unique event. He was also a bard and the son of another called Hoarvien who appears to have been a Druid. In fact so does Hervé.

As a Christian figure Hervé was patron protector of horses. As a Druid hailing from Leon where the vice is hereditary he was automatically a horse thief. A strange quality in a religious man. A local doggerel runs:

sant Hervé Mene Bré
Laer an noz, laer an de
sant Hervé Mene Bré
Laer ar c'hezeg noz ha de

Saint Hervé (of) Menez Bré
Stealer of the night, stealer of the day
Saint Hervé (of) Menez Bré
Steals horses night and day

According to tradition Hervé was also blind, an inhibiting factor
in a horse thief one must suppose, and one day he confronted Kian
on the mountain and tried to convert him to Christianity. The Druid
replied that if Hervé persisted in his gospel chatter he would curse the
Church and all the Christian chapels would fall down and the congregations would perish. This badly shook Hervé and he left Kian to his
'paganism'.

On 17 June, within a few days of the summer solstice and the feast
of the sun god Belenus, a prayer at Saint Hervé's little chapel on
Menez Bré will cure skin diseases in horses. If you bring a crippled
child to Kian's spring near the chapel he or she will be cured. So it
seems the two holy men were at last at peace with each other, which is
as it should be.

Hervé's horse thievery and the blindness of both monk and Druid
is strange imagery and the implication has been lost. But the area
around Guincamp — 'the white settlement' — is alive with strange
customs passed off as Christianity, but senseless within the context
of that religion.

At Plouegat-Moysan, a very small town halfway between the
Menez Bre and Morlaix there was an annual religious festival rather
like a Roman orgy. All through the night were wrestling matches
between local champions, drinking, dancing and bagpiping. After
the sun rose the young men and women took off their clothes, or the
rest of their clothes, and plunged into the spring. The Church looked
on benignly and called all this a cure for rheumatism. Unfortunately
in 1855 the local mayor banned the festival, describing it as 'a disgusting exhibition contrary to public decency'. It has never been held
since.

Another curious story survives at Saint Jean le Doight — 'of the
finger'. Here is preserved what is said to be the index finger bone of
John the Baptist, the skull of Saint Meriadek, and an arm bone of
Saint Modez. These relics are paraded around a bonfire at the
summer solstice.

There is a story about the saint's finger bone. Anne of Brittany was
resting at Morlaix when she heard of the famous relic, and its power

to cure sore eyes. Having a pink one she sent for the bone but the reliquary had disappeared. Anne had the guardian monk flogged then left Morlaix in a rage. The following day the finger bone was back in its normal place. The explanation of the mystery, or rather the moral of the story, is that the finger wants itself used only to cure the illnesses of humble folk. The monk's views are not recorded.

It is odd to hear of Meriadek described as a 'saint'. At Lanrivoare in North Finistère there is a mass grave for the 7,777 victims slain by one Meriadek the previous owner of the Saint Jean skull. In the churchyard there is a plaque to this effect, which gets it wrong in the French translation underneath. '*Seiz mil seiz kant siez ugent ha seiz*' in fact means 'Seven thousand, seven hundred, seven times twenty (*ugent*) and seven, which comes to 7,847 so seventy of the slain are commemorated twice but this is by the way. Meriadek was supposed to have been a fifth-century pagan chief who hated Christians. The victims are described as 'saints' on the plaque so even in the fifth century Brittany could out-saint Rome.

Plouegat-Moysan to Saint Pol de Leon is a sore road, deadly with fast and gigantic lorries burning the oxygen from the air to the cross-Channel ferry at Roscoff. But I love Saint Pol and I had to walk there out of respect. My seven years in Brittany had associated the city with home-coming or home-going. I was always pleased to arrive there on my way back to England and happy to be back after crossing from Plymouth.

For me Saint Pol has the boisterous camaraderie of London's old Covent Garden, for Leon is the market garden of Brittany. There is magic in the pink soil of Leon for the vegetables grow faster and bigger here than in the Garden of Eden. While spring vegetables are gasping their way to the surface or elsewhere, the Leon vegetables are already waiting in the soft sun. Thousands of hectares of them, potatoes, great artichokes like Martian thistles, cauliflowers and, of course, onions.

The Leonais are big people, lighter haired than the rest of the Bretons, businesslike, shrewd bargainers but at the same time generous. They will get the last centime for a cauliflower then make you a gift of two more, and such cauliflowers that you are proud to hold them in your arms. But on the other side of the coin they are realists. It's difficult to get a passage for your car on the ferry for England when the market price is right and the crop ripe. The highest priority for the Leonais are convoys of vegetable lorries.

The syndicate which owns the ferry is the same one that markets the crop so it's no use protesting that you are British and better not be trifled with. At such times it's far better to go and see the local tanks of live lobsters and crayfish, fellow Britishers on their way to a grimmer fate. But you'll get on the ferry eventually, and the bistros and restaurants of Saint Pol are jolly and friendly and I'd say that the Leonais understand the British personality as much as any foreigner can. And not a few of them speak English so well that you wonder whether Saint Pol is more a part of England than France.

Most of us have met one of these English-speaking Bretons. In Leon they call them 'johnnies', in Britain we call them 'Brittany Onion Men' and 'Henri' even 'Bill' and 'John'. They answer to any name, these merchant princes of the beret, bicycle and onion string and they have been calling at British homes for generations.

One of my earliest recollections of them was arriving home just in time to prevent my mother, who was unworldly, from buying a bicycle off a 'johnnie'. He had already sold her most of the onions in Leon and judging the market to be a seller's one he thought he'd do her the favour of selling her the bicycle as well.

He left with his bicycle, still friendly, saying he'd be back sometime. I remember his parting shot:

'Eh, alors, your muzzer would not like a ket, would she?' I said we had several 'ketz' and wanted no more. But he didn't mind, and shook my hand. I miss him now.

I met several 'johnnies' and descendants of 'johnnies' in the small bistro by the side of the level-crossing at Saint Pol. Nothing more typifies the innate politeness of the Bretons than the way they will stop speaking Breton, which they know you can't understand, and recommence their conversation in French, which they think you might. But they knew me so they didn't bother. A little tip. The word to use in a Breton bistro is '*Yechedmad*'. It is worth dozens of '*à votre santé*' or '*tiens-tiens*'. Another English trait is that they play dominoes in the bars. I don't know why more Englishmen do not spend more time at Saint Pol instead of rushing off the ferry at Roscoff and dashing south.

Saint Pol was once called Kerleon and still believes it really is the chief city of Leon, not Landerneau, probably with some justification. Geoffrey of Monmouth wrote that Kerleon, he spells it Caerleon, was King Arthur's Court. Sir Thomas Malory, himself a medieval knight and fifteenth-century adapter of Chrétien de

Troyes, in his *Morte d'Arthur* mentions Caerleon in a different context. 'Here lies Arthur *rex quandem rex futurus*.' When his land is in dire peril Arthur and his knights will awaken from their long slumber and come to her aid. A strange thing is that one of the most common surnames in this corner of Brittany is Arthur.

Saint Pol-Aurelien, who gave the city its modern name, arrived in the sixth century and came like Gildas and Samson, from Saint Iltud's monastery in south-east Wales. The legend says that he became chaplain to King Marc'h after slaying a dragon on the Ennez Batz, the island just offshore from Roscoff. There he built a monastery.

Now Arthur steps into the picture, or maybe he does for a variation of the legend says the defender of Kerleon was Wither, which would be pronounced 'Uther', Arthur's father according to Geoffrey of Monmouth. A siege ensues and Kerleon is razed to the ground by the Saxons. No Arthurian victory here. When the city was rebuilt it was named for Saint Pol. But there seems to have been a squabble between Marc'h and the saint for he tried to have his confessor poisoned, a poison that did not take effect owing to the intervention of God.

At the cathedral lie the remains of some of the old kings of Leon. One is Konran Meriadek, pagan mass murderer at Lanrivoare, and saint according to Saint Jean le Doight which has his skull. Skull collecting seems to have been the fashion for the cathedral has several boxes containing the skulls of chieftains, each neatly labelled with the name of the owner.

There is a curious reminder of the Druids in the legend about the spring of Saint Pol — or '*Feunteun Paol*' as it is called in Breton. The story goes that when Saint Pol arrived at the ruined city the only life he found was at the spring and these were animals, a bull, a wild boar with her young, and a hive of bees. According to the pamphlet issued by the Church the legend is symbolic of the spiritual degeneration of the inhabitants of Leon before conversion to Christianity. In fact nothing could be further from the case provided one doesn't accept the Christian view that it is the only religion. All three are Celtic deities and worshipped by the Gauls.

I have spent a long time at Saint Pol, the chief city of Tristram and of the legendary country sunk by British historians off the coast of Cornwall. But war horns are blowing in the mist and all is savage tumult and outrage. To the south the Saxons were attacking the hill of Agned and we must fight Arthur's eleventh battle. We went by train.

9   Hill of Agned and Badon

The *Menhirs* — the standing stones of Brittany — act differently for different people. They awe, do nothing, walk down to the river to drink, dance, or make humming noises. All these things have been attributed to the vast megalithic monument at Carnac and the kind of performance depends on one's sensitivity or imagination.

For most people the puzzle of Carnac is a practical matter — how thousands of vast pillars were sculpted, dragged into position, then raised on end by a primitive unmechanical people some four thousand years ago? According to a nineteenth-century archaeologist a hundred men with ropes, pulleys, and wedges, barely moved one of the stones a few centimetres in a long day's work. To my view this person had found the answer he was seeking but couldn't see it. He was unconsciously thinking in modern terms of manpower and time — in fact he was costing the operation. But the erectors of Carnac — just as their successors had built walls by a couple of stones at a time — did not think in terms of cost. They would be content with a few centimetres a day, and the next, and so on for eternity. In today's terms of cost no-one in their right mind would think of erecting a pyramid, a Great Wall of China, even a Hadrian's Wall. But these feats of prehistoric endeavour are not marvelled at for the inspiration but for their extent.

The real riddle of the stones lies not in practicalities but in the kind of inspiration that moved the builders to put them there. Between the Etel and Auray rivers at Carnac are not only Menhirs, but cromlechs, burial mounds and passage graves stretching as far as you care to look. In fact the trouble with seeing Carnac is that it is dwarfed by its own immensity. Stonehenge is like this. You have to move so far off to appreciate the scale that the stones seem small and insignificant. There are so many stones that once it was doubted that they could be accurately counted and mapped, indeed it was believed that sorcery was at work, that 'evil' forces did not want the stones fooled about with. But there can be no doubt that Carnac is the largest religious site in the world, a holy or 'white' region compared to which Saint Peter's at Rome or Saint Paul's at London are but parish churches.

We know of no comparable faith today, and what's more seem to doubt that prehistoric man could have had one either, strange in a civilization which still builds temples to deities of one kind or another, great buildings of a spiritual rather than a practical value.

One wonders if there were no written records of Jesus Christ, and our churches were deprived of writing, what an archaeologist of, say, the year A.D. 6000 would make of a cathedral. Christian churches are orientated so that the altars are towards the east. This would suggest to our future archaeologist that we worshipped the rising sun. The tombs of the dead are probably the debris of some ghastly ritual sacrifice. And we used bells to drive off evil spirits. Stranger still there are idols, men and women with wings and the chief figure seems to be a young man nailed to a wooden structure who appears to be dead. Perhaps our archaeologist of the future might conclude that the entire edifice was dedicated to an early aviator killed while attempting to fly a very primitive flying machine. Maybe we are in danger of making this kind of mistake about sites like Carnac.

There are almost as many theories about Carnac as there are stones. French humorists, most of whom consider Bretons to be a low water in human intellect, have suggested that the arrangement of stones was an unsuccessful attempt by the original Bretons to build a stone wall. Then Carnac could be a Stone Age long-range practical joke of the genre: 'I know it took a lot of time, Glug, but we've nothing else to do and I laugh myself sick when I think of their puzzled faces in 4000 years' time.'

A more serious view is that the arrangement, like that of Stonehenge, can predict seasons. At least some of the alignments coincide with the rising of the sun at the end of the first weeks of November, February, May, and August, the beginnings of seasons important for sowing, germination, ripening, and harvest. If this is so then they also coincide with the four main Druidical feasts of Samain, Imbok, Beltane, and Lugnasad.

Between the ludicrous and the practical we have the metaphysical, most of them to do with petrification. They are Roman legions turned to stone for killing Christians. They are, some of them, the petrified disciples of Saint Cornely, an imaginary pope said to have been martyred in A.D. 253. They are groups of dancers, male and female, for the imaginative can see men's and women's shapes in the stones, turned to stone for dancing on Sunday. This tradition of petrified dancers occurs so frequently at ancient stone circles that one wonders if this can be a folk memory of a dance ritual once performed at them.

The tradition about Saint Cornely and his petrified disciples is particularly interesting. In the region of Carnac there are numerous chapels dedicated to him despite the fact that not only was there no such pope there almost certainly was no such person. In Brittany he is the patron saint of horned beasts and he is always depicted in church statuary and banners in company with a bull. His name comes from the old Gaulish word for 'horn' and for the pre-Christians he was the bull god, and perhaps something more.

The Celts worshipped him under the name 'Cernunnos'. A famous representation of him is on the silver Gundestrup bowl, stolen in antiquity by Saxons and found in a Danish peat bog at the end of the last century. Here he is depicted with deer antlers on his head and obviously not the horns of domesticated beasts. For the Celts, perhaps, he was Lord of the Hunt. There is another local tradition at Carnac. At certain times of the year, particularly the spring, it is said, the stones run with blood. It was these kinds of thoughts that have set me wondering whether by coincidence I got a glimpse of one use to which Carnac was put.

I lay in the shade of one of the great stones, too long maybe, for it had grown colder. Such is the spell of Carnac that as the sun begins to die and the stones draw long shadows the tourists begin to hurry away and leave them in peace. The grassy meadows are low and already a mist was rolling in from the Morbihan, the 'little sea'. But I didn't want to move. My hotel would be full, hot and noisy. Here at least was peace.

I was disturbed from my reverie by a sound. I thought at first that it was the skylarks for something seemed to have got into them and they had been fighting like tom cats all day. I had heard the car doors slamming and thought everybody had gone but now I could see there was a party of children still playing in and out of the stones in an impromptu hide and seek. The stones lent themselves admirably to the game.

From my vantage point the stones marched down in two double

columns to a large stone table called the 'slaughter stone' about a hundred metres away. The hide and seek had formed itself into two groups — the hunters and the hunted. Suddenly the hunted broke from their hiding places and raced up the slope towards the slaughter stone, screaming as they ran. It was now less a flight than a panic for there were screams of terror instead of laughter and chatter.

My imagination saw crowds of warriors lining the stone forest and driving the human sacrifices back into the centre of the arena. And the hunters with spears beating along the stones, flushing them out, driving the prisoners up to where the Druids waited to drag them to the altar. Those too terrified to run were slaughtered against the pillars. Perhaps what I saw in the sobbing, terrified children was the ritual hunt of Cernunnos to propitiate the spirits of the chase. It had a strange effect on me and I can't forget it.

That Carnac is full of Druid 'dragons' is sure for it is under the protection of the angel, Saint Michael, and also the Holy Trinity, the most powerful spiritual quartet in Christendom. Penmarc'h was bad enough but the Christians were even more worried about this 'white region'.

The Church is forever complaining about black magic vandals despoiling church property, but one wonders what kind of arrogance — perhaps it was fear — prompted the nineteenth-century assault by Christian vandals on Carnac. It seems that any curé or monk with time to spare went to Carnac with a team of labourers and pulled down a stone or two. Only the immensity of Carnac saved it from complete destruction. As in the case of Penmarc'h the task was too great so the Christians had to content themselves with chiselling crosses on some of the more accessible stones and placing puny crosses on their summits. It was a peashooter versus elephant operation and the Powers of Darkness have prevailed.

A curious custom hereabouts is 'ar mel beniguet' — 'the blessed hammer'. Most of the chapels have them, or had them, polished stone hammers which look remarkably like those found at sites attributed to the New Stone Age. A person near death and in pain makes the sign of the cross before 'the blessed hammer' to gain relief. Within living memory the ritual was even more realistic. The sufferer was tapped three times on the head with the stone. Maybe further back in time the skull was cracked open with it, an antique form of euthanasia.

The old Celts were quite ruthless with tribal chiefs too frail with age for usefulness or wisdom and there was an annual slaughter of them at the Feast of Samain. The curious ceremony at the death of a pope where his head is tapped three times with a small silver hammer may also be a survival of this savage ritual.

The mist was quite thick now and Carnac is not a happy place to be after dark. My mind was full of *ankous*, head-tappers, and stones running with blood as I made my way to the main road. A vast white shape swam at me from out of the mist. 'Ding-dong, ding-dong, dong-diddy-ding-ding-dong,' it cried. Then I heard a human voice calling: 'Chocolate glacées ... chocolate glacées.' 'feesh-cheep, shreemp-vinkle,' it shouted in final desperation. I am a sucker for the kind of enterprise that tries to sell ice cream at a deserted and ghost-ridden site in the darkening mist so I walked over to what I could now see was a white van which appeared to be eating a man with its bonnet.

'Thank God,' said the man, withdrawing his head. He had a sad thin face and a white cap with '*Monsieur Fruti*' on it. 'I thought you would never hear me. Do you know anything about engines?' I knew enough to see that the terminals of the starter battery were badly corroded. It was the work of a few minutes to clean them with my knife. The engine started immediately and '*Monsieur Fruti*', real name Jean-Pierre, offered me a lift to Auray.

I remembered the 'feesh-cheep, shreemp-vinkle' cry and asked him how he had known I was English. Jean-Pierre told me that before he became 'Monsieur Fruti' he had been an attendant at the aquarium at Concarneau and was an expert in recognizing the different nationalities of the visitors. He had prided himself in talking about his fish in the appropriate language hence 'feesh-cheep' and 'shreemp-vinkle'. I secretly wondered how Jean-Pierre had come to associate edible commodities with the live things in his tanks, but I couldn't ask him for the sad face had seen a lot of suffering. Probably he had learned the expressions from an English tourist with a sense of humour.

'Ding-dong, ding-dong, dong-diddy-ding-ding-dong,' sounded Jean-Pierre at a gendarme on a bicycle. In the rear mirror I could see the gendarme dismount and take our number.

'*Tant pis*', said Jean-Pierre, almost smiling. 'It is the law of France to go "pon-pon" when you overtake someone. My "pon-pon" is wired up to my "ding-dong" so that's what he gets, like it or not.' I wasn't very happy all the same for we were returning to the district where probably I was on the police files. I could see them at brigade headquarters, crying out in the harsh accent of Gauloises and garlic: 'He is back, *le sacré Anglais*, I have seen him, the relentless dumper of red tennis shoes and stealer (*incorrigible*) of ladies' knickers by act of dog.'

Jean-Pierre enquired politely why I was going to Auray, *'en vacances'*, perhaps? I told him rather rashly that I was looking for King Arthur. I did not mention that I had him in the back, plus a monk and a bard, amongst the ice cream cones and wafers but Jean-Pierre almost lost control of the van. Arthur the king he did not know, but he knew well Arthur the Octopus. He was the husband of Hortense the Octopus. He had kept them in a tank at Concarneau and he loved them so much that it had got him dismissed.

According to Jean-Pierre, Arthur and Hortense were strange and introspective, most times lying inert in their tank, bored and motionless. Jean-Pierre had worked out that it needed an audience of exactly five to bring them to life.

One — no good, two — nothing, three — not a movement, four — complete indifference. But five. Whing, Arthur and Hortense shot about the tank like aquatic spaghetti. They gambolled and played, rolled in the sand at the bottom, and presented each other with bouquets of seaweed.

I commented that it was strange that octopuses counted in fives, eights would have been more likely. But Jean-Pierre did not joke about octopuses and said that although my remark showed that I had an alert mind it was irrelevant. Five was a magic number for those octopuses. Six spectators and they short-circuited, sank down to the rocks, lying there like old shammy leathers. This presented a problem for Jean-Pierre. Only when there were five spectators would Arthur and Hortense eat their 'shreemp-vinkles'. But as soon as they started to eat they drew a crowd exceeding the magic five and they became inert once more.

Jean-Pierre began to hate the crowds, for far from loving the octopuses as he did, they loathed them. According to him they pulled faces and made sick noises like 'yeck, yoelk, yerk' then went to fetch their friends who, when they saw Arthur and Hortense, cried out, '*Quelle horreur*' and '*Dégoûtant*' and also went 'yeck, yoelk, yerk'. Finally it became too much for Jean-Pierre to bear.

On that black day they were vulgar people from the slums of Paris, gross and loud, said Jean-Pierre through clenched teeth. His eyes turned to black beads and his face wrinkled like a prune. There were five of them and Arthur and Hortense were skyrocketing about their tank eating 'shreemp-vinkles' and playing. Then it started as it always did.

'*Quelle horreur*' and '*Dégoûtant*'. went the Parisians. 'Yeck, yoelk, yerk.' 'Fetch Henri, and Mimi, and petite . . .' But for Jean-Pierre the hour had come. He stopped them.

'One moment,' he said. 'When you see the *merde* of a dog on the pavement, you do not rush off to get your neighbours so they can go 'yeck, yoelk, yerk'. You ignore it. You go away. Why do you behave like that with my octopuses? If you don't like them, if you loathe them, if they disgust you . . . piss off.'

The Parisians had, but to the office of the *directeur* who had told Jean-Pierre to piss off in his turn. And this is how he became '*Monsieur Fruti*'. This was the sad story and I could imagine the octopuses waving him a sixteen-armed farewell. I wanted to ask him how Hortense's husband came to be called Arthur but now he was thinking of his lost friends and was uncommunicative.

Auray is a pleasant little town on the Auray river but it gets buried under the thousands of tourists that arrive at the Morbihan after the *Grand Départ* in mid-June and becomes a residential supermarket with the locals acting as if they had been rubbed over with sandpaper. The Alrées are renowned for their pigheadedness and sharp tempers. According to Breton lore they are born with the temperaments of devils and on top of this mass tourism sours people. They want the prosperity but they don't want the bother and they get angry.

It was in an Auray gift shop window that some years ago I discovered one of my valuable sources of reference, an old map of Brittany on the sleeve of a long playing record. I was copying the map into my notebook, surely a harmless enough theft, when the owner burst out of the door to say that if I wanted to know the tunes on the record 'also for nothing' then he'd be overjoyed to whistle them for me. I thanked him for his kindness and said that if a hole for this hypothetical record were required I was quite prepared to punch one in his face. But he declined the offer and withdrew.

The cathedral is named for Saint Gildas and the stained glass illustrates scenes from the saint's life, mostly puff and vanity and bad for an old gentleman like my companion. The artist doesn't seem to have known much about his life for he is not shown writing his famous 'complaining book' — the only known contemporary account of the Dark Ages. Maybe this was not spectacular enough but he can't be forgiven for overlooking the story of Saint Gildas and the devils.

Gildas was writing in his cell when he was interrupted by seven monks who came to say that his mentor, the hermit of the island of Flatholm, was dying. They had come to fetch him so he could pay his last respects to the old man whom he loved.

There was something about the monks that Gildas did not quite like. When he spoke to them of God they hurriedly changed the subject, strange for holy men who normally spoke of little else. So the saint decided to put them to a test. Producing his catechism from his trunk of books he commenced to read and the 'monks' suddenly vanished, and so did the boat for that also was a creation of their master, the Devil. This left Gildas floating in the middle of the *Mor Briezh*. If you saw a nude monk sailing a trunk across the English Channel in A.D. 540 then probably it was Saint Gildas. Climbing aboard his trunk and using his crosier as a mast and his habit as a sail he successfully voyaged to Flatholm just in time to administer the last rites to his old master.

The Kerzo swamp to the north of the town and east of the Auray river is an historic killing ground. Charles de Blois, pretender to the dukedom of Brittany, was slain here in 1364 together with most of his 3000 men-at-arms and archers. At exactly the same spot 431 years later during the Revolution 952 Royalist troops were shot to death by the *sans-culottes*. According to the locals, on dark nights when the wind blows hard from the sea the swamp echoes with the agonized cries of the dead. And I don't blame them for a similar wind brought a strike of mosquitoes through my bedroom window.

There are more winged stingers in the Morbihan than in the rest of Brittany put together. At dusk you wonder what the strange noise is. It is like a gale blowing through telephone wires. You soon find out. The swamps about here make a fertile breeding ground for the brutes and my experience at Saint Guinox was light relief compared with the furious attack by the Auray squadrons. Maybe this is what makes the Alrées so irascible.

Youenn Nicolazic was working on his small parcel of land to the north of the Kerzo swamp when he saw the apparition of a beautiful lady bearing a lighted candle. Then the vision faded. Later he began to see her everywhere but when he told his friends they thought he had crabs in the head and had better lay off the wine. The manifestations continued and the madman became the object of much scorn and derision. Two years later however, on the 25 July 1624, he was with some friends when the lady appeared. She announced that she was Saint Anne, mother of the Blessed Virgin. She beckoned and they followed.

Saint Anne led them to the top of the hill. Here a thousand years earlier, she said, once stood a monastery dedicated to her but it was destroyed by the Saxons. The stones of which Nicolazic's barn was built and those of his friends came from the ruined monastery. To repay her she told them to build a chapel on the same spot. Then she vanished.

Such a task was clearly beyond the means of a poor peasant and the churchmen he told did not believe him. But exactly one year later while digging at the site Nicolazic found an ancient wooden statue of Saint Anne. After this small miracle the church no longer thought that he was a madman or rogue and they treated him with respect and honour. On Nicolazic's hill they built a chapel as Saint Anne had wished. Now the town of Saint Anne has become the most important place of pilgrimage in the whole of Brittany, says the local guide book.

Strange then that Saint Anne was not included in the *Tro-Briezh*, stranger still that the town was called Keranna long before 1625 and before there was one building on the hill it was named Ana or Agned, the '*Mamm goz ar Vretoned*' — 'the old mother of the Bretons', the earth-mother herself, just like the lovely hills in County Kerry. The 'hill of Agned' was Arthur's eleventh victorious battlefield.

While searching for 'the hill of Agned' scholars have debated at great length the meaning of '*Cat bregion*' which occurs as an alternative in some versions of the Nennius manuscript. In Old Welsh '*Cat*' clearly meant 'battle' but '*bregion*' was a mystery even when the last syllable was docked for it is obviously monkish interference with a Celtic word. '*Breg*' also meant nothing but '*bre*' was '*hill*' but then it began to be asked why a manuscript, as parsimonious of words as a Red Indian chief, has troubled to include both descriptions, as the original must have done, an unnecessary repetition that it was 'a battle of the hill'.

I can make an original contribution to the debate. '*Breg*' is not Old Welsh for 'hill' but Gaulish or Old Breton for 'swamp'. Perhaps the original manuscript would have read, I can only surmise this, 'And the eleventh battle was at the hill of Agned and was called the battle of the swamp'. Four kilometres west of Agned is the village of Brec'h which took its name from the kind of terrain on which it was built, the vast area of swampland which included Kerzo.

There was no folk memory of the warrior Arthur but there was certainly one of a mighty battle fought by Saxons about 'the hill of Agned'. The prize would have been the monastery which the Christian legend of Saint Anne had used for the miracle. One would have dearly loved to have seen the old wooden statue of the saint. I am sure she would have not been wearing a Christian halo. The statue of the mother goddess found at Cirencester, in fact three statues of her for she is a triplicate of goddesses as nearly always in Celtic mythology, has the figures holding trays of food, most likely vegetables, fruit and loaves. Unfortunately the Agned idol was publicly burned during the Revolution.

I was far from happy as I set out that morning to walk the ten kilometres to Badon. For I knew I could be proved badly wrong in my belief that Arthur's battles were in fact fought in Brittany. The town of Baden had only changed one letter from Badon in fifteen hundred years. This was a positive identification, there was no alternative that could be used with honesty, and Nennius had specifically stated that this battle had also been fought on a hill.

The prognosis was doubtful. The hotel-keeper had said that he could not recall the town being on a hill. I had countered that motorists do not notice hills like walkers but he had shaken his head. The coast of the Morbihan, as he had picturesquely and unkindly described it, was 'as flat as a nun's chest'.

From the start it did not look promising. The land was well wooded and I could not see further ahead than the next clump of trees. To my left lay the Rival Sal and a marsh. I could hear the marsh for the wind sucked up by the burning sun rattled the reeds like dry bones. To my right flat cornfields extended to the horizon. Beyond Badon I knew there was definitely low ground called dismally Brec'h Pen an Toul — 'Devil's Head Marsh'. Then there was the sea.

I still don't know why the Morbihan attracts so many tourists in the summer months unless of course it is the discotheques and the ice cream parlours. There are no beaches to speak of, only sand brought there on lorries. There is dangerous sailing to be had amongst the islands of the 'little sea' but the wild life, apart from the mosquitoes, has been shot out of existence. My grandfather was mainly responsible, that's if the figures in his game book can be believed.

My grandfather was amongst the sportsmen who came annually to the Morbihan for duck shooting. The Victorian view of what constituted sport seems to me to be the kind of flagellation that might have appealed to Saint Gildas. His journal is full of imminent disaster but couched in such cool terms that one wonders if they were the same kind of people. The craze was for punt-gunning. Loading a small cannon with black powder and shot they cast themselves loose in these shallow craft into the fog banks of winter. The current is strong and the object was to drift downstream into a raft of feeding ducks. A yank on the gun cord, a fearful explosion, and there was terrible slaughter, not only of the ducks, for not infrequently the cannon exploded and killed the punt gunner.

In case of survival there was always great difficulty in picking up the bag for the corpses drifted on down with the current to be collected by wily Bretons lurking in the reeds. The difficulty now was to explain that the ducks were your property. These wild marshmen did not speak French — certainly not my grandfather's French — and the dispute usually ended with the gentlemen having to buy back the ducks they had shot.

But by far the greatest hazard was the difficulty in making one's way upcurrent again to find the parent yacht, particularly in the fog. On one occasion my grandfather was swept out into the Morbihan and was not recovered until a day later. He was covered with ice but survived. Some unfortunates were actually taken out through the arms of land which shield the Morbihan into the open Atlantic. These were seldom found alive. But it was all great fun and no doubt the survivors enjoyed talking about it over whisky and soda in their clubs.

Then I found the road begin to rise perceptibly and I was shaken from my reverie of Victorian fortitude by a church spire pointing above the trees. Finding that Badon was actually on a hill had the same effect on me as entering an old cathedral. I felt something close to ecstasy.

There was something quite special about Arthur's last victory. Tight-lipped Nennius breaks into a literary canter on only two occasions in his description of the twelve battles. The first was over Arthur's eighth battle at Castle Guinnion of which he says:

'Arthur carried on his shoulders an image of Saint Mary Ever-Virgin and there was great slaughter of the Saxons, through the strength of our Lord Jesus Christ and the Holy Mary, his maiden mother.'

The second was the final occasion, for according to the monk Arthur fought only twelve battles and the last was at Mons Badonicus. Nennius wrote:

'The twelfth was on Mount Badon, in which — on that one day — there fell in one onslaught of Arthur's, nine hundred and sixty men; and none slew but he alone, and in all his battles he remained victor'.

An early Welsh source, the *Annales Cambriae*, gives us some more religion and uses the magic power of three:

'The battle of Badon in which Arthur carried the cross of Our Lord Jesus Christ, for three days and three nights, on his shoulders, and the Britons were victorious'.

Judging by this example Arthur seems to have become a reformed character since the time he was attempting to scrounge Saint Padern's shirt.

For Saint Gildas Badon was a turning point in history for, according to him, the battle was so decisive that when he was writing his 'complaining book' peace had reigned for forty years and the Saxons were not normally peaceable people.

Why this should have been so has been the anvil for much scholastic hammering, the common view being that Badon was so disastrous for the Saxons that for a time they gave up all hope of further expansion, even fleeing the British Isles. A widely quoted source which gives support to this view was written about A.D. 865 by 'a monk of Fulda' who even asserts that the ancestors of the continental Saxons, living today in Germany's Saxony, spring from what he called the 'Angli' of Britain. Chased out of Britain the Saxons recrossed the North Sea to Haduloha — Cuxhaven today — and offered their services as mercenaries to Theuderich, King of the Franks, who at the time was at war with the Thuringians.

To my mind this concept of a military disaster on such a scale in a Britain almost completely under Saxon domination is incredible. A Celtic victory at Bath in Somerset, Badbury Rings in Dorset, Badbury in Wiltshire, Badbury in Northamptonshire, and Baumbar in Lincolnshire, all put up by various authorities as the place of the famous battle, certainly would not stampede the Saxons across occupied Britain to row to Germany. This would be as likely as a footballer failing to score and dribbling the ball back through his own team to put it into his own goal. Another disqualification of the supposed battlefields is that their names almost certainly came from a legendary Saxon hero named Badda. Gildas and the rest were Celts and it seems most unlikely that the site of the massive Celtic victory would be named after a Saxon warrior. Disregarding this disqualification we are still looking for a place where a purely local defeat would bring peace for at least a generation. Brittany's Badon is such a place.

Badon was a Celtic hill fort and you can still see the seaward defensive ditch. It stands on a narrow strip of land which runs from the sea between marshland thus barring the route to the interior. A Saxon force landing in one of the creeks would have to gain control of Badon before marching on to the glittering prizes of Auray and Vannes. If, thanks to Arthur's army, the Saxons were unable to capture the fort, an assault which ended in costly failure, then there would be no alternative to a mad dash back to their boats and the sea. A defeat would drive the Saxons out of Brittany.

I can see them rowing miserably back up the coast, their hopes dashed. They feared Arthur for he had already defeated them or their bloody brothers-in-arms all along the coast from Tribruit around the wolf's head to Badon. They must find a landfall that would accept a beaten army. But where? Northern Gaul was barred to them. There is real historical evidence that the Saxons were badly beaten by the Franks in a great battle in A.D. 486 and that the home side became the masters of northern Gaul, thus diverting a stream of prospective Saxon invaders from Gaul to Britain. They would not be welcome in Britain for it would be the case of Saxon meeting Saxon and plunderers do not get on well with plunderers. But the Franks needed reinforcements for their war and Theuderich took them in.

My Badon has another point in its favour. By no stretch of the imagination could Gildas not have known the hill fort. His own monastery — not Bieuzy's — stood on one of the arms of land which embrace the Morbihan. He would have had to pass through the fort to go inland to Castennec or anywhere else to slay dragons. So the monk who first told the world about the great victory at Badon lived for at least some of his life within eight kilometres of a place with the same unusual name. This could be coincidence but it's too big a one for me.

Lacking a boat you can get to Rhuys by walking round the Sarzeau peninsula. By doing so you must pass through Arzon which the
locals believe is named for the great warrior called Arzur who once
lived in a fort in the Sarzeau forest at the time of Gildas the monk.
Local tradition has Arthur actually buried on the tiny Morbihan
island of Gavrinnis, just offshore from Rhuys. On the island is the
most beautiful passage grave in the world. The carvings on the interior face of the tomb are so splendid you weep inside. The patterns are
in a form which defies the modern intellect to grasp them. The con-
centric spirals seem to beat out a rhythm which you can feel rather
than see, and to describe them would be like trying to describe music
to someone who has never heard it.

It is a tomb fit for the greatest warrior in history. Owing to a confu-
sion of translation French authorities believe that 'Gavrinnes' means
the 'island of the goat'. In fact it means 'the island of the giant' and
the locals believe that the tomb was built for a giant. Arzur the bear
god was supposed to have been a giant. But I do not believe our
Arthur was buried here. It has never been called Avalon or 'the Isle
of the Blest'. And I knew a more likely spot where I'd like to bury him
and I'll do it later.

When Gildas first came to Brittany he lived on an island called
Houat just off the Morbihan. According to his biographer, Warok
the chief and father of Trephine, Conomor's father-in-law, came to
the monk and asked him to build a monastery at Rhuys for the good
of the souls of his tribe. After much hesitation Gildas agreed.

Gildas's monastery no longer stands. The original was destroyed
by the Saxons and another built by Geoffrey, Duke of Brittany, at
the beginning of the eleventh century. An abbot of the monastery
sometime during the next century was Pierre Abélard, the great
lover of Héloise, the nun. Abélard hated Rhuys and considered himself an exile from Paris although he was a Breton by birth. He doesn't
seem to have understood the language for he described his Breton
monks as beasts and their language beastly.

Later on, like not a few religious houses, Rhuys fell victim to the
religious madness called 'Pelagianism'. One of the abbots, fed up
with being middle man, decided that he himself must be God. The
monks sold the church plate and took to a life of drunkenness and
whoopee which, when the news reached Rome, got them all excom-
municated and eventually the monastery fell down. It was never
rebuilt.

The monastery was never famous but is interesting for one of those mind boggling asides made from time to time by monk chroniclers so you have to read it again to see if you have got it right.

'When the Saxons came,' wrote an anonymous monk of Rhuys, 'the monks fled the raiders and took with them the most priceless treasure of all, the Holy Grail brought to Brittany by Joseph of Arimathea.'

From history we know that these monks fled to the Benedictine monastery of Saint Benoit-sur-Loire but there is no record there of the famous chalice quested so long by King Arthur and his Knights of the Round Table.

The stone tombs from the abbey were later transferred to the church which is all that survives of Gildas's monastery. Behind the altar are three of them. They belong to two of my companions. Saint Gildas had come a long way for such an old man and he needed rest. So I said good-bye for the last time to the red faced, crusty old monk, the first chronicler of Arthurian times, although he never mentioned the mighty warrior. He lies at Rhuys now. So does Bieuzy.

I also said farewell to Arthur for he had to leave for the marshes just south of the River Glein, where he was to fight the fatal battle of Camlann. I did not want to be there when it happened. I would like to remember him as I had first met him in the dolmen in the Landes de Lanvaux, not a bloody wreck in the mists of Camerunn, not far from Saint Nazaire.

Taliesin and I marched with Arthur back to Badon. The warrior chief was sad with the presentiment of Death. But like a good Celt he knew that Avalon was no purgatory. In the Halls of the Slain he would meet his old comrades. Then there would be feasting, fighting and loving. He'd even get even with Lancelot, each day and every day for eternity. He hitched his great round shield higher on his shoulder, grasped the spear called Ron more firmly and padded off down the narrow dusty road.

'Kenarvo, Arzur,' called Taliesin.

'See you again, Arthur,' I called.

The warrior halted at the bend in the road, withdrew Caliburn from its scabbard and waved the great sword three times over his head in the final Celtic farewell. Then he was gone.

10   Slow Train to Avalon

The fewer the clues the wider the circle of suspects and this is particularly true of Avalon, Arthur's final resting place. Nennius is mute on the subject and Geoffrey of Monmouth tells us next to nothing and that is all we have to go on.

The great warrior dies, Geoffrey says as the result of treachery. Arthur is marching on Rome but hears of a revolt against him by his faithless nephew Modred — Medraut according to Welsh legend. He meets him at Camlaun at the head of a combined Saxon and Celtic force and a great battle is joined where most of the loyal Celtic nobles perish, Arthur received his mortal wound and is borne away to the Isle of Avalon to be cured but to no avail. He dies leaving his crown to a kinsman. Later Geoffrey adds that the location of the island is 'in distant seas' and is also called the 'Isle of the Blest'.

Avalon is supposed to come from the Celtic word '*Aval*' meaning apples'. I disagree for this is a clear case of scholarly unthink. Windswept islands are notoriously unproductive of high vegetation of any kind let alone fruit trees. Avalon does not come from 'apples' or '*avalou*' but from the more reasonable word 'winds' which is '*avelou*'. In Celtic legend, particularly Irish legend, The Isles of the Winds figure prominently together with The Land of Eternal Youth and The Field of Happiness as nice places to go when you die.

A strong candidate is Belle Isle which lies off the Morbihan and about fourteen kilometres by sea from the Quiberon peninsula. It is an old Druid burial ground and also a place of mysticism for tradition holds that the great cave on the north end of the island was a healing temple. It is called the Cave of the Apothecary. The island is guarded by dangerous reefs, off-liers of the islets of Glazic and Valhuac and also those of Gildas's Houat. There are two safe channels to the island called respectively 'the passage of the Blest' and 'the road of the Blest'. So we have all the ingredients. A cave where

Arthur is said to slumber to await the call to save his country, a healing temple where they tried to cure his wound but failed, and a hint that it might have been called at one time 'The Isle of the Blest' from the names of the channels through which the boats bearing the dead must have passed. Enough strong winds blow across the island to qualify the island for 'Isle of the Winds' and it is not too far from Camlann, just over sixty kilometres away by land and sea.

I would not have Arthur buried there for worlds. It has a large prison, popcorn, discotheques, hundreds of 'Monsieur Fruties' and 'kiss me quick' paper hats. But I must confess that I had already found something far better. I had almost run into it when I was blundering about the Chenal du Four in the fog when I first arrived in Brittany. I could never forget that great hump of wild rock. I wanted Arthur's Avalon to be there.

My Isle of the Blest was off the coast of Leon and the nearest railway station was at Brest, one hundred and sixty kilometres in a straight line from Auray. But the Société Nationale des Chemins de Fer had made sure there was no straight line from Auray. The train wandered off to Quimper, meanwhile zig-zagging between towns and hamlets in a way which suggested that the driver was either looking for Arthur himself or that he was writing a guide to the bistros of rural Brittany.

The Bretons have a story of such a train. A guard was summoned to a compartment by a lady who told him that if the train did not speed up she was likely to give birth. The man was aghast, protesting that the lady should not have got on the train in that condition. The lady replied that when she had boarded the train she had not been in that condition.

But the prolonged journey will give me time to tell you about the kind of warrior Arthur might have been, a warrior who according to Nennius had slain nine hundred and sixty Saxons single-handed. The Saxons had their 'berserks', now a word that means madness, but the original 'berserk' was a man who could slay fifteen men or more, not man by man but in a body. The Celts had them too. Arthur was such a man but we don't know any more about him than I've told you in this book. But he was like the Irish hero figure called Cu Chulain. He will serve our purpose.

There are two versions of how Cu Chulain came to be. In one he is the son of the god Lug. In the other he was born three times to three different families all noted for superhuman qualities. 'Cu' means 'dog' in Irish Gaelic and he was given the name when at the age of seven he slew the watchdog of Culann the smith, a hound of such rapacity that the owner gave him horseshoes for dinner. But the killing was a bad thing and as a penitence Cu took on the job of guardian of the kingdom of Ulster.

But until the age of seven Cu was no prodigy, like any other Celt of noble family being farmed out to foster parents for his education. According to the hagiographers this is precisely what had happened to the young future Saint Gildas who was said to be the son of Caunus, 'a most noble and Catholic man'. But instead of a hermit who lived on Flatholm Island Cu received his tuition from Amairgin the poet, and from Sencha, Fergus and Cathbad, no doubt other Druids, who taught him wisdom, warfare and magic, to fit him for the role of guardian of his people.

The Celtic hero figure is essentially violent and uncouth. The Welsh hero Culhwch thundered into King Arthur's Court on horseback. Cu announced his arrivals at the court of the king of Ulster by dashing to the ground the chessboard at which the king was peacefully playing. He gained his bride by a kind of courtship which resembled rape. He wins his knightly spurs by telling lies, cheating, and mayhem.

Cu grew into a handsome man, so said the bard, but he cancels this out with Celtic enthusiasm. Or maybe the fashion of beauty has changed. This hero had seven pupils in each eye, seven fingers on each hand, seven toes on each foot. His cheeks were like rainbows, red, yellow, blue and green. His long dark hair was of three colours, black at the roots, red in the middle and white at the ends. He loaded himself with jewels, a hundred strings of beads were in his hair, a hundred gold ornaments at his breast.

His appearance was quite normal, said the bard no doubt taking a mighty swig of metheglin while he thought what to say next. His audience would expect the butterfly to change into a tadpole. But, he continued, you should see him in his battle frenzy. Cu's body was seized with mighty contortions. He confused the enemy so they did not know whether he was retreating or coming at them by turning around in his skin. His feet and knees shot to the rear and his buttocks to the front. Flame jetted from his jaws, black blood spurted from the top of his head, and his hair stood on end and crackled and burned like fireworks. One eye receded into his skull and the other dangled down on his cheek. His face lit up like a beacon.

In this state Cu's fury was uncontrollable and after battle he had to be plunged three times into icy pools to cool him down. The names of the heroes who formed the fire brigade have not come down to us but there would be no rush for the job. One listener might ask what all the other warriors of Ulster were doing while Cu was fighting the other four provinces single-handed. This did not stump the bard for a moment. He told them how all the men of Ulster were cursed into menstruation on the day of battle and had to lie down.

Cu too had his problems for he was constantly at war with his *geisa*, the bardic literary stumbling blocks which made him do what he was forbidden by taboo to do. One said that he must not pass a cooking hearth without eating food. Another said he must not eat the flesh of dogs. So on his way to the great battle he passed three sorceresses who were rustling up a dog for lunch. By eating a shoulder of dog Cu's prowess was diminished.

Although Amairgin had taught Cu to be the greatest poet in the world he was forbidden to recite a poem. So next he encounters a wily Druid who challenges him to a rhyming battle, satirizing him unmercifully until he is enflamed into replying in like fashion. Another of his *geisa* is broken and great wounds spring open in his body.

Washing his hurts in a lake Cu is horrified to see an otter drinking his blood. He kills the animal before he remembers that his last exploit would involve the killing of a dog just as his first had. The Celtic name for an otter means 'water dog'. So he knew his end was near. In his death agony he chains himself to a Menhir and defies the enemy until his last gasp. So Cu is slain by sorcery, for though he is unbeatable he must in some way be beaten in a way which leaves his reputation unsullied. Arthur had to die, not in normal battle with the Saxons in which he is unconquerable and supreme, but by the intervention of witchcraft for Medraut had consulted a sorcerer on the way to Camlann.

On leaving the train at Brest I fell victim to one of those flashes of repartee for which the French are famous. The ticket inspector on the train who had found me an apple after I had complained of thirst and refused payment was standing at the ticket barrier as I left. I gave him what I thought was a franc for a glass of wine. Something made me turn and he was gazing hard at the coin, palm outstretched as if petrified like one of Carnac's Sunday dancers. I was seized by fear. I have a Gallo-Roman silver coin which rather stupidly I keep loose in my pocket. Immediately concluding that I had mistakenly handed it to the inspector I hurried back to retrieve it. But I was wrong. I had given him one of those useless old aluminium centimes, a kind of Mickey Mouse money that you get in your change in France and never seem able to foist off on somebody else.

'I thought, *monsieur*,' he said in his nasal Parisian accent, 'that you had returned to collect the interest.'

From Brest I caught the bus to Brignogan for I wanted to walk down the coast, the muzzle of our wolf, to my Isle of Avalon. Somehow it seemed the reverential thing to do. This stretch of coastline is as iron-bound as a sea shanty. Across the frightening Chenal de la Helle is the great snaggle-toothed rock that we know as Ushant and the French call Ouessant. This stretch of sea is majestic with strong tides and overfalls and it is a good place to steer clear of with an onshore wind. Here the Atlantic meets the English Channel and wrestles with it.

It is said that at one time the local population entirely existed on the proceeds of salvage from wrecks that came ashore through failure to keep clear of Ushant. And it was also said that not a few of the shipwrecks were by design rather than accident. The locals attached lanterns to the horns of cows and hoodwinked mariners into thinking they were somewhere else.

So great was this menace that during the last two centuries the locals sold a kind of insurance. For a tidy sum a shipowner could buy *brefs de sauvetage* so that in the event of shipwreck the cargo would be protected from pillage. The shipmaster was advised to keep the papers on his person for the *'pillards'* invariably searched corpses when they were washed ashore. This kind of arrangement seems open to all kinds of abuse but they say it worked quite well.

The coastal villages south of Brignogan are full of strange stories about ancestors who were horses, or who had horses' heads. This may be a survival of the Gaulish horse cult found at Penmarc'h and also in the white horse cut in the chalk at Uffington, Berkshire, England which is believed to have been executed by Belgic settlers about one century before Jesus Christ. At the largish village of Saint Fregant they say that not only did their ancestors have horses' heads but they are descendants of Phoenicians from North Africa. Scholars have explained that this tradition might come from the fact that Caesar brought a troop of Arab cavalry with him to these parts. He certainly mentions Africa and 'Silicia Namgidde' seems an odd name for a Roman citizen.

One wonders if it can be mere coincidence that the old lords of the area had for their coat of arms a silver horse's head. Oddly, the name of the oldest recorded family was Marchec which means 'little horse'. One is either lost in the baffling ethos of Celtic mythology or the explanation might be more prosaic. Brittany used to be the largest supplier of horses for the tables of France.

I marched along the coast road to the extreme western tip of Brittany — to Aber Wrac'h, the 'bay of the witch'. This great bay is reminiscent of a Norwegian fiord and in winter is as cold. Thanks to the almost perpetual onslaught of the westerly gales the country is bleak and almost devoid of trees. Even the few that manage to survive have been trained by the wind so that their branches point towards the east. Unlike Lervily the cottages do not face south but have their backs towards the west — a trait which you notice in the locals for when they stop to gossip they automatically turn inland. It is here that one can fully appreciate that the Breton concept of a cold hell is infinitely more discouraging to wickedness than a hot one.

Most impressive about the coast from Portsall to Laniltud are the offshore lighthouses and buoys, flashing winking beacons marking lonely rocks in the dark sea. This is the area of silent fog klaxons and invisible lights. Maybe the phantoms of dead 'pillards' are up to their trickery with cow lights.

High on the steep cliff above an *aber* is the village of Laniltud, named for Celtic history's most famous abbot, Iltud, tutor in Wales to Gildas and Samson and, so says tradition, four hundred and twenty other 'saints'.

Welsh legend starts Iltud off as a prince of the Cymri, the original inhabitants of Wales, a great warrior and sage. He became one of the super-warriors who guarded the Holy Grail. When he forsook the sword for the cowl his successor was Arthur.

The Welsh have Iltud as Welsh. The Bretons say that he was a Breton who went to Wales. To put this in some kind of proportion it is only fair to say that the Breton hagiographers also lay claim to the patron saints of Wales, Ireland and Scotland — David, Patrick and Andrew. The only patron saint not owned by the Bretons is George of England. He was a fair hand with the dragon but he would be a Saxon and anathema to the Celts.

Plouarzel is a small village a couple of kilometres away from the cliffs. Here, says local tradition, came the silver bier bearing the body of wounded Arthur or Arzur as he is called locally. He lay there three days and three nights while word was sent to the Isle of the Winds for a ferry to carry him over. Then they came for him in a white boat rowed by oarsmen in total white. But Plouarzel is a dangerous place for embarkation, the cliff is steep and the seas murderous. The place where the Druid dead began their last voyage to the Land of Eternal Youth is near Point Saint Mathieu.

Today this most westerley point of France is called Finistère which is a later translation of the Latin — *Capus finis terrae*. The Romans ignored the Gaulish name for this place. It was, and still is in Breton, Pen ar Bed. Unlike the French or Roman names it does not mean 'the cape at the end of the land'. It means 'the end of the world'. It was just that for the dead because they started their marvellous journey to the islands towards the setting sun.

From Pen ar Bed you can just about see the Isle of Avalon. Even on modern charts it is called Enez Beniguet — The Isle of the Blest — as Geoffrey of Monmouth had called it. It is long, low, and dark against the white of the rip tides. This is where I'd like Arthur to be, asleep in his cave amongst the sea thrift and the sobbing winds. You can't get there, and maybe if I could I wouldn't. Let him slumber in peace.

Who was King Arthur? Can we make the real King Arthur stand up? It is very unlikely and my journey, apart from personal contentment and a strong belief that I had followed Arthur too, has contributed nothing towards that end.

Arthur may have been a memory of the bear god, a legendary personification of the giant Celtic deity known for cunning and strength, fine attributes in a pre-gunpowder warrior. He may have been Taliesin or Saint Iltud for nothing is really known of either except that the legends have both as mighty warriors before they got bored with it. Or Saint Gildas.

It seems odd that the monk indirectly responsible for the birth of Arthur failed to mention his name, a strange oversight in a tale of a battle which saved the Celtic world, or at least held back the Saxon darkness. As far as Brittany is concerned Gildas is often associated with Arthur's battlefields as we have seen. Did he omit his own name from the account purely out of modesty? Unlikely, but just as likely as the theory that he left out Arthur because he had slain his brother. Gildas never held back when naming the Celtic chiefs who fornicated while the Celtic world crumbled. Surely Arthur would have got a tart reference somewhere in the famous 'complaining book'.

What about the terrible Conomor as a candidate? He also turns up like bad news at Arthur's battles, or rather Gildas's victories. Conomor only means 'the big chief' so we don't know his real name. There is so much we don't know.

There has even been a speculation as to who Gildas's adversaries actually were. Picts from the north have been suggested. Gildas seems to have been more than a little daft and in his mind all was horror with demons springing at him from the darkness of evil. Not on one occasion does he specifically mention the Saxons. They were 'the enemy'.

Intriguing in this respect is Caesar's complaint that the Venetii invited reinforcements from the British Isles. Geoffrey of Monmouth states that Arthur took his army to Gaul. Could Gildas have been describing the destruction of the homes of the Venetii after the great defeat at sea? Were the reluctant chiefs, who are absent from British historical records and with one exception, Maelgwyn of Gwenedd, from Welsh legend, in fact other Gaulish chiefs who did nothing while the Romans mopped up the patriots. It bears thinking about.

On the theme of history jumping to the wrong conclusion why do the Bretons believe that they came not from Britain but from the east? The strange impression that their forebears were half men and half horses seems comical but it has an historical parallel. The wild horse warriors who swept west from Asia dismounted so rarely that their victims actually believed that they were fifty-fifties.

Using one of these horses to get back to the theme of the identity of Arthur from which I seem to have galloped I am personally persuaded that there is a very good chance that Arthur was a cavalryman after all. The Saxon galleys could travel far swifter than marching men, taking short cuts across estuaries and bays. Arthur would have had to keep up with them, meet them when they landed. The only answer would have been horsepower. As I have said earlier in this book if Arthur did march then he would have been the exception for the Celts loved their ponies as much as their metheglin. Maybe Arthur's superiority came from fighting as cavalry the Saxons who were essentially foot soldiers. Back to my theme.

More likely Arthur had no real identity but was a portmanteau character used by the bards to carry all kinds of stories. As a stock character the bard's listeners would know what to expect of him. The teller could get to the nub of the yarn without tiresome explanation about the personality of the hero.

The method is common to tales of all great folk heroes from Hereward the Wake (*Normans Go Home*), Robin Hood (*Rob the Rich to Feed the Poor*), through to Daniel Boon (*We're just Plain Folks but We'll Fight for the Liberty of our Great Land, Yessireebob*), and Ned Kelly (*No Joker's Going to Push Us Around, Mate*). The technique used today with television heroes. Nobody has to first explain what a tough softy Telly Savalas is.

But I've got a confession. I am King Arthur. Or maybe you are King Arthur. King Arthur could be any one of us. Arthur is 'the once and future king'. When the reincarnation happens Celtic magic would consider it a quibble whether Arthur is English, Scottish, Irish, Welsh, French, American, or Japanese for that matter.

It is best that Arthur remains an enigma for he can be all things to all men. For some he is trumpets, banners, coats of arms, tournaments with horses pelting up the lists, shining armour, damsels in distress, chivalry, and righting wrongs. And let it be faced, his cuckolding by Lancelot and the rest makes him a gentleman and a high-powered mug.

My Arthur is no fool. He is no gentleman but a rogue, a rowdy slap-and-tickler, a money-borrowing, crafty boozer. I'm sure his men would have called him 'Archie' or 'Art'. He is the wind in the trees in summer, the taste of good whisky, the moment of joy in sadness when you hear a crowd singing 'David of the White Rock', he is what you feel when you know a great hulking Breton fisherman has walked through the village with a bunch of flowers for your birthday, or at the New Year when he gives you back the same cigar you gave him the previous one.

All kinds of Arthur live still in those wonderful stories about him, from the *triads* through Chrétien de Troyes, Malory, Tennyson, Scott, Laurence Binyon, E.A. Robinson, Comyns Carr, Symons, Hardy, Masefield, Charles Williams, Alfred Duggan, T.H. White who unkindly has him as a Saxon, Anya Seton, and Rosemary Sutcliffe with her beautiful theory about how Arthur got his horses. Enigma Arthur may be but we still write about him fifteen hundred years after his death. We love him, warts and all.

I stood on the high cliffs over the Chenal du Four with Taliesin. It would be the last time I would see him so clearly. The wind ruffled his white robes and blew fingers across his harp making silver music.

'He's coming now,' he said. There was a great rush of wind over-head and I could see lights burning on the Isle of the Blest.

'Kenarvo', he said softly and strode away through the heather. He would return to the church of Saint Gildas for with Bieuzy he lies beside the monk. I was content. Arthur was in his Otherworld, Gildas in Heaven, and Taliesin had gone back to his shadowy planet in the constellation of Apple Pie. And I? I thought I'd go and have a final drink with the 'johnnies' before I caught the ferry for England.

Amberley, Sussex